CW00763486

The Double Crisis of the Welfare State and
What We Can Do About It

DOI: 10.1057/9781137328113

Also by Peter Taylor-Gooby

NEW PARADIGMS IN PUBLIC POLICY

A LEFT TRILEMMA: Progressive Public Policy in an Age of Austerity

SQUARING THE SPENDING CIRCLE

REFRAMING SOCIAL CITIZENSHIP

WELFARE STATES UNDER PRESSURE

RISK IN SOCIAL SCIENCE (*with Jens Zinn*)

LEARNING ABOUT RISK (*with Jens Zinn*)

IDEAS AND WELFARE STATE REFORM IN WESTERN EUROPE

NEW RISKS, NEW WELFARE: The Transformation of the European Welfare State

MAKING A EUROPEAN WELFARE STATE? Convergences and Conflicts in European Social Policy

WELFARE STATES UNDER PRESSURE

RISK, TRUST AND WELFARE

EUROPEAN WELFARE FUTURES (*with Vic George and Giuliano Bonoli*)

THE END OF THE WELFARE STATE? Responses to Retrenchment (*with Stefan Svallfors*)

CHOICE AND PUBLIC POLICY: The Limits to Welfare Markets

EUROPEAN WELFARE POLICY: Squaring the Welfare Circle (*with Vic George*)

MARKETS AND MANAGERS (*with Robin Lawson*)

DEPENDENCY CULTURE (*with Hartley Dean*)

SOCIAL CHANGE, SOCIAL WELFARE AND SOCIAL SCIENCE

THE PRIVATE PROVISION OF PUBLIC WELFARE (*with Elim Papadakis*)

PUBLIC OPINION, IDEOLOGY AND THE WELFARE STATE

FROM BUTSKELLISM TO THE NEW RIGHT

SOCIAL THEORY AND SOCIAL WELFARE (*with Jen Dale*)

POLITICAL PHILOSOPHY AND SOCIAL WELFARE (*with Raymond Plant and Harry Lesser*)

DOI: 10.1057/9781137328113

palgrave▸**pivot**

The Double Crisis of the Welfare State and What We Can Do About It

▶

Peter Taylor-Gooby

University of Kent, UK

DOI: 10.1057/9781137328113

First published 2013 by
PALGRAVE MACMILLAN

Palgrave Macmillan in the UK is an imprint of Macmillan Publishers Limited, registered in England, company number 785998, of Houndmills, Basingstoke, Hampshire RG21 6XS.

Palgrave Macmillan in the US is a division of St Martin's Press LLC, 175 Fifth Avenue, New York, NY 10010.

Palgrave Macmillan is the global academic imprint of the above companies and has companies and representatives throughout the world.

Palgrave® and Macmillan® are registered trademarks in the United States, the United Kingdom, Europe and other countries

ISBN: 978-1-137-32812-0 EPUB
ISBN: 978-1-137-32811-3 PDF
ISBN: 978-1-137-32810-6 Hardback

This book is printed on paper suitable for recycling and made from fully managed and sustained forest sources. Logging, pulping and manufacturing processes are expected to conform to the environmental regulations of the country of origin.

A catalogue record for this book is available from the British Library.

A catalog record for this book is available from the Library of Congress.

www.palgrave.com/pivot

DOI: 10.1057/9781137328113

Contents

List of Figures

DOI: 10.1057/9781137328113

DOI: 10.1057/9781137328113

Preface

Most people agree that the British welfare state faces problems. This book follows the guiding principle of much academic research: why let something be difficult when with careful reflection you can make it seem impossible? It also seeks to be positive.

We identify two crises: first, the immediate crisis resulting from the 2010 government's decision to respond to the longest recession for over a century by the deepest and most precipitate cuts ever made in social provision in this country plus a massive restructuring programme affecting nearly every area of public provision. Second, the long-run crisis of rising costs due to population ageing, insistent wage pressures and rising aspirations in the big-spending welfare state services of health and social care, education and pensions.

The first crisis is compounded by policies which direct the harshest welfare state cuts to benefits and services for those of working age, particularly affecting women and families, and by the restructuring of the NHS, social care, local government, the education service and all benefits apart from pensions. This will fragment national services, greatly expand the role of the private for-profit sector and intensify work pressures. It is hard to avoid the impression that some, at least, in government are seizing an opportunity to implement policies which deepen social divisions and undermine the contribution of common social provision, symbolised by the NHS, to social cohesion. One objective is to embed the cuts permanently. Another is to

DOI: 10.1057/9781137328113

advance a larger programme to shift the political economy of the UK towards a radical, competitive and individualistic liberalism.

The second crisis exerts more gradual but equally insistent pressures on the more popular mass services, health, education and pensions, which have escaped the most stringent cuts in the immediate crisis. The two crises are linked because it is the popularity of the mass services that leads the current government, committed to spending cuts, to concentrate those cuts on services and benefits for poor minorities. If extra money is not found in the longer term, the continuing growth of demand for resources in the more popular areas will squeeze spending targeted on the poor even further.

One obstacle in the way of attempts to promote more humane and generous welfare is the 'welfare state trilemma': the three goals of designing a generous, inclusive system, ensuring it is effective in meeting the challenge of the double crisis and winning an election are hard to reconcile, especially when the platform includes higher spending on welfare. British voters dislike tax increases; the majority believe that the poor are work-shy.

The book argues that a viable and humane programme is possible and that current circumstances offer an excellent opportunity to start implementing it. Welfare for those of working age rests almost entirely on stigmatic means-testing that separates out claimers from others and endlessly questions their willingness to work. Substantial progress has been made in developing proposals for more inclusive policies that treat them as past or potential contributors to society with normal aspirations for work and family life. Such policies involve considerable extra spending and could be introduced only in stages as the link between entitlement and social contribution is established in the public mind.

There are indications that the public would accept extra spending to address poverty among children, who cannot be seen as responsible for the circumstances they find themselves in, and for adults who take responsibility for their lives. About three-fifths of people below the poverty line live in households where there is at least one full-time earner. Much working-age poverty is a problem of low wages, not of shirking. Social investment, preventative policies and 'pre-distribution', centred on higher minimum wages, could raise incomes at the bottom and reduce the costs of redistributive welfare to help mitigate working-age poverty.

The incidence of poverty among children is higher than among adults. The sums involved (0.7 per cent GDP to end child poverty at current

DOI: 10.1057/9781137328113

levels) are large but not impossible, being about one and a half times the increased spending on benefits for children during the past two decades. Further resources to kick-start social investment programmes in child and elder care and to start developing contributory welfare among working-age adults might come from a reduction in the 1.1 per cent of GDP accounted for by tax relief on non-state pensions. The experience of shared inclusive provision that emphasises social contribution and common aspirations for family life will also help shift public attitudes towards support for more humane and inclusive policies, while heavily regulated continually work-tested provision marks down claimers as scroungers who must prove otherwise. In this sense generous welfare builds its own constituency.

In relation to the long-run crisis, the experience of the past two decades is that sustained pressure to raise productivity has enabled health and education spending to keep pace with wage pressures. Projections by UK and European agencies show that the problems in the long-run are again not insuperable, equivalent to raising an extra 0.4 per cent of GDP in tax each decade for half a century. State spending in these areas has in fact risen at roughly twice this rate during the past three decades. Spending on private schools, clinics, medical insurance and pensions has also risen sharply. People value health care, education and pensions, are prepared to pay for them and presumably will continue to do so. The real question is whether the extra money will support better national services or unequal, divisive and ill-co-ordinated private systems. Further problems arise in ensuring all social groups can get the same access to the best schools and colleges, and that health care outcomes are more equal. Specific additional targeted measures could raise standards for the most vulnerable. Additional regulation for the private welfare state, directed largely at better-off groups, will also help promote cohesiveness and equality.

These reforms are affordable if introduced over time by a determined government. The next question is how to ensure public support. The major social changes of recent years result from three processes: women participate in paid work on a footing more nearly equal to that of men but are more heavily burdened with child and elder care; education, training and skill are much more important in determining opportunities in work and in a world where income inequalities are stretching out; and people live more flexible family and working lives, so that it is harder to safeguard against risks and insecurities in losing a job, needing to provide care for a frail relative or meeting sharp rent increases. The emergence of the new

DOI: 10.1057/9781137328113

social risks that affect people during working life not only challenges the welfare state but also provides new constituencies of support for collective social provision. The common need for these services and the inability of the non-state sector to provide them for those on low and middle incomes is increasingly obvious, especially during the current crisis, when insecurities affect more and more people. New risks affect particular groups at specific life-stages. An effective political platform for the welfare state would need to draw together a range of interests in relation to education, training, child and elder care, low pay, working conditions and employment protection and link this with the child poverty and social contribution programmes outlined above.

The response to the double crisis set out in this book involves real increases in state expenditure: Britain would eventually move back to its previous position at the middle of the group of major industrialised countries ranked by government spending, rather than falling to the bottom. A reforming government would need to confront the interests of the winners under the current policy regime, and of newly entrenched commercial service providers. It would face opposition in raising wage levels for those on the lowest incomes and in implementing more stringent regulation of private and charitable providers. However, the levels of spending in question are feasible because they follow the trend to the expansion of welfare state spending during the turbulent period of the past three decades, under a variety of governments. The newly important needs for child and elder care, education, training and opportunities, affordable rents, decent wages and more say in the workplace bridge across a range of social groups and rally a coalition of support for the programme. The double crisis is being used by the current government to justify abandoning the commitment to a generous and inclusive welfare state and shifting to market liberalism on the US pattern. It also provides the opportunity to construct a realistic programme which might take Britain in a very different direction.

This book would not have been possible without help and advice from a large number of colleagues. Particular thanks are due to the Leverhulme Trust, which generously supported the work with a Fellowship, to Ben Baumberg, Kate Bell, Hartley Dean, Nick Ellison, Ian Gough, Andrew Harrop, Gavin Kelly, Colin Hay, Martin Seeleib-Kaiser, Jane Lewis, Richard Scase, Gerry Stoker, Trude Sundberg and Win van Oorschot, who generously commented on various drafts, to my bike, for taking my mind off things, and, as always, to my family.

DOI: 10.1057/9781137328113

List of Abbreviations

BIS	Department for Business, Innovation and Skills
CCG	Clinical Commissioning Group
CBI	Confederation of British Industry
CPI	Consumer Price Index
CQC	Care Quality Commission
DH	Department of Health
DWP	Department for Work and Pensions
EC	European Commission
ECB	European Central Bank
EU	European Union
GMG	Glasgow Media Group
HoC	House of Commons
IFS	Institute for Fiscal Studies
IMF	International Monetary Fund
IPPR	Institute for Public Policy Research
NAO	National Audit Office
NCVO	National Council for Voluntary Organisations
NI	National Insurance
NICE	National Institute for Health and Clinical Excellence
PFI	Private Finance Initiative
PPP	Public–Private Partnership

DOI: 10.1057/9781137328113

OBR	Office for Budgetary Responsibility
HCPAC	House of Commons Public Accounts Committee
HCPASC	House of Commons Public Administration Select Committee
PISA	Programme for International Student Assessment
RPI	Retail Price Index
SCIE	Social Care Institute for Excellence
VAT	Value Added Tax
WBG	Women's Budget Group

DOI: 10.1057/9781137328113

palgrave▶**pivot**

www.palgrave.com/pivot

1
The Double Crisis of the Welfare State

Abstract: *The British welfare state faces a double crisis: immediate cutbacks in response to the recession bearing most heavily on benefits and services for those on low incomes, especially women and families, and longer-term pressures on health and social care, education and pensions from population ageing and other factors. Government decisions to focus the cuts on the most vulnerable exacerbate the first crisis. Policies which fragment and privatise the main state services in response to the second undermine the tradition of a universal welfare state. The cuts are deeper and more precipitate than any among comparable developed economies or for at least a century in the UK.*

Keywords: cuts; double crisis; fragmentation; liberalism; population ageing; privatisation; retrenchment; welfare state; women

Taylor-Gooby, Peter. *The Double Crisis of the Welfare State and What We Can Do About It.* Basingstoke: Palgrave Macmillan, 2013. DOI: 10.1057/9781137328113

The welfare state, the idea that a successful, competitive, capitalist market economy can be combined with effective services to reduce poverty and meet the needs people experience in their everyday lives, was the great gift of Europe to the world. Now it is under attack and it is a war on two fronts. The conflict is experienced with especial severity in the UK. The response to the 2007–8 banking crisis, repeated recessions and economic stagnation in this country has been to balance budgets by cutting government spending rather than increasing taxes. The harshest cuts are in social provision, with the poorest groups bearing the brunt.

Standing behind the immediate attack on the welfare state is a second crisis, which now attracts rather less attention in policy debate. Projections of the numbers likely to use the main welfare state services (health and social care, education and pensions), of future wage levels and of other factors indicate that the costs of maintaining, let alone improving, provision will rise steadily during the next half-century. Taxpayers will have to pay more or accept lower standards.

This book addresses the double crisis of the welfare state with a particular focus on the UK. It shows how the immediate and longer-run pressures interact. The second, slow-burn crisis sets the mass of the population against more vulnerable minorities. The high-spending expensive services, such as health, education and pensions, are top priorities for most people. Spending on the less popular benefits and services that redistribute to the poor is steadily eroded. The government's response to the immediate economic crisis builds on this division, cutting the redistributive benefits to maintain the big-spending mass services. The fact that this is happening in a context of growing inequalities and social divisions makes the task of developing a humane and generous, effective and politically feasible response to the double crisis that much harder.

In this chapter we examine the twin crises in more detail. Chapter 2 considers how they interact and analyses their impact on the politics of state welfare. Chapter 3 examines the problems faced in making a case to sustain and improve provision in the current context, focusing on redistributive welfare for the poor. Chapter 4 extends the discussion of feasible, effective and humane policies to health and social care, pensions and education. Chapter 5 brings these arguments together, evaluates the opportunities for more generous and inclusive directions in policy and identifies the political forces that might be harnessed to drive them forward.

DOI: 10.1057/9781137328113

The immediate crisis: recession, cuts and restructuring

Britain's welfare state is unusual in a European context in being financed mainly through taxation rather than social insurance payments from employers, workers and government. Tax finance presents the question of who pays in and who gets the benefits more directly and raises immediate issues of stigma and desert. The system includes high-quality and relatively cheap mass health care, pensions at modest levels, an average education system that achieves good results for those at the top but not for others, relatively extensive (but costly) social housing, and weak provision for those on low incomes, with limited skills or who are vulnerable for other reasons. The main division lies between the universal services that meet the shared needs of the mass of the population (health care, education and old age pensions) and those directed at poor minorities (unemployed, sick and disabled people, lone parents, those who can't afford rents and families in low-waged work). It is here that questions of desert arise and that entitlement tends to be policed through means-testing and stringent work tests.

Britain's response to the economic crisis is also unusual.

The 2008–9 recession was the deepest since at least the great crash in the 1929–31 and has already lasted longer than any previous recession for

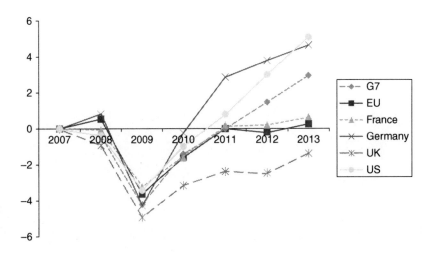

FIGURE 1.1   *GDP change as percentage of 2007 GDP, 2007–13*
Source: Author's calculations from IMF (2012), projected from 2012.

DOI: 10.1057/9781137328113

at least a century. Figure 1.1 shows the pattern of economic growth across the two major comparable European economies, France and Germany, the EU as a whole, the US and the G7 group since the start of the first recession in 2007. G7 includes the largest established capitalist economies: the US, Canada and Japan as well as the UK and France, Germany and Italy and offers a global comparison. The graph plots the decline in GDP and shows how long it took to return to the pre-recession level. The collapse in 2009 was of between 3.5 and 5 per cent of GDP. All of the countries and groups of countries had recovered to their 2007 level of output or surpassed it by 2011, apart from the UK. Germany, the US and the G7 then continue to grow, while France and the EU as a whole stay at about 2007 levels. At the time of writing, some 60 months after the onset of recession, the UK is still struggling to return to its previous position. It is not expected to do so for at least another year.

The UK has, effectively, lost the resources that would have been produced over the period since 2007 if output had simply stood still. One outcome has been a real fall in living standards for most people as wages fail to keep pace with price rises, about 7 per cent between 2009 and 2013 for those on median incomes (Joyce 2012, 15). So far as the welfare state goes, the response of the incoming coalition government in 2010 was to cut state spending radically, although as Figure 1.2 shows, spending

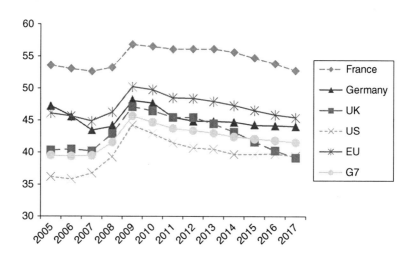

FIGURE 1.2   *State spending, major economies, 2005–17 (per cent GDP)*
Source: IMF (2012), projected from 2012.

DOI: 10.1057/9781137328113

in the UK was already at the average of the G7 and much lower than in the other major European countries or the EU average in the better times of the early 2000s. The graph shows how spending has already fallen sharply. On current plans it will continue to decline even when the economy recovers. This pattern differs from those elsewhere. Most countries tend to stabilise state spending close to or slightly above pre-recession levels when resources return. In the UK, spending will sink further below European spending levels to fall beneath those in the G7 by 2014–15 and in the US by about 2016–17. This marks a decisive shift in the level of government involvement in society and in the economy. The UK has not spent a smaller proportion of national resources on public services than the traditionally market-centred US during the period of more than a century for which good records are conveniently available.

The cutbacks are combined with an equally profound programme of structural change. We consider the two aspects of reform, cuts and restructuring, separately.

The cuts

The 2010 government set itself the objective of eliminating the budget deficit by 2014–5, revised to 2017–18 in 2012 as economic growth failed to return (HM Treasury 2010, 2012b). The programme set out in the 2010 Spending Review envisaged massive and rapid cuts in public spending, about £100bn in all, including about one-fifth of the £166bn budgeted for housing and community, environmental protection, law and order, defence, economic affairs and other public services in 2010, and about 18 per cent of the £105bn budgeted for welfare for the poor, housing benefit, unemployment and family benefits and for disabled people (HM Treasury 2010). The target for benefit cuts was raised to 22 per cent in 2012. By contrast, the government chose to protect the mass welfare state services (health, education and pensions) which account for about 60 per cent of state spending. These experienced relatively minor cutbacks in current spending, although capital spending plunged headlong, by three-fifths for education and one-fifth for health services (IFS 2011, 138, Chowdry and Sibieta 2011, 4). The decision to ring-fence current spending on the more popular services resulted in much greater damage to benefits for low-income people and to less popular areas of state provision.

DOI: 10.1057/9781137328113

The cuts accounted for some three-fifths of the resources required to balance the budget and tax rises (mainly a legacy from the 2005–10 government) some two-fifths. They included a rise to 50 per cent in the top rate paid by the 2 to 3 per cent of tax-payers with incomes over £150,000 (cut to 45 per cent in 2013), a rise in National Insurance contributions for all employees of 1 per cent, and an increase in the mildly regressive VAT, plus a one-off banking levy, a rise in Capital Gains Tax (later reversed) and increases in alcohol and fuel duty.

The cutbacks coupled with immediate stimuli intended to promote a return to growth, such as the 2009–10 car scrappage subsidy, cuts in corporation tax and other taxes on business, further tightening of public spending, and £375bn of 'quantitative easing' (whereby the Treasury encourages private sector lending by increasing the availability of money to banks), failed to prevent a further slide into recession in 2011–12. By 2012, Office for Budgetary Responsibility projections indicated that the budget deficit would not be eliminated until after 2017–18 and that there is little hope of extra buoyancy to compensate for the lost production of the years of recession (OBR 2012a, table 1.2). The government remains committed to further cutbacks focused again on short-term benefits and local government, in an attempt to stimulate private sector led recovery.

This programme failed to achieve its goals of reducing the deficit and stimulating growth. Further cutbacks in benefits were introduced in 2013, with £5bn diverted from public services to investment in infrastructure and a cut in corporation tax to 21 per cent, the lowest rate since the tax was introduced in 1965 (HM Treasury 2012b).

Cutbacks on this scale are exceptional in British policy-making and have been much discussed (for example, Crouch 2011, Gamble 2011, Gough 2011a, Skidelsky 2012). Here we outline the government's underlying assumptions, examine how the cutbacks are structured to achieve a specific impact and consider the risks run in pursuing these policies.

Assumptions underlying the cuts: In recent years most governments in developed economies have pursued economic policies that balance two underlying approaches. Those inspired by Keynesian counter-cyclical theory see the problems of economic downturn in terms of the resources (factories, people, investment capital) that lie idle. They argue that government must make up for the contraction in private investment. This can be financed by borrowing, which temporarily increases indebtedness but can be paid off out of the proceeds of future growth. An alternative liberal approach argues that the long-term solution must rely on

DOI: 10.1057/9781137328113

competitiveness in international markets and hence on low public deficits and free markets providing good investment opportunities to attract private capital. The latter view is more appealing to those who believe that there are structural weaknesses (as they see many of the restrictions on market freedoms) in national economies that currently damage competitiveness and that may now be corrected.

Both viewpoints have influenced policy in developed countries, but the balance has shifted more in the liberal direction as stagnation has continued (Skidelsky 2012, Crouch 2011, Davies 2010). Figure 1.2 shows that the response to the second recession of 2011–12 (the slight upswing in state spending in those years) was much weaker than that to the first recession in 2008–9. The UK is the leading exponent of liberal economic remedies, cutting spending harder and faster than any of the major developed economies, indeed than any European economy apart from those compelled to do so as a condition of IMF, ECB and EU loans.

Structure and impact of the cuts: The UK cuts are indeed exceptional. Roughly two-thirds of government spending is directed at welfare state provision, in order of scale: the NHS, pensions, education, other cash benefits including housing benefit and benefits for disabled people, social care and social housing. The remainder is spent on the military, police and prisons, the rest of local government (apart from education, social housing and social care), transport and environmental policies, again in order of spending. This complex interactive mechanism disposes of about a third of GDP, of everything that all economic activity in the country generates in a year. The cuts affect all areas but are not spread evenly. Non-welfare services lose roughly a fifth (IFS 2011, figure 6.3). When it comes to the welfare state, the cuts are targeted away from the most expensive and popular areas which are used by large numbers of voters, such as the NHS, education and pensions. Instead they are concentrated on the rather lower spending but less popular benefits and services for lower-income people of working age: benefits for low-paid, unemployed and disabled people, for families and children, and for housing.

The cuts will save about 27 per cent of planned spending on disabled people of working age (some £16.4bn) through reforms to employment support allowance, the replacement of disability living allowance by the less generous personal independence payments and more stringent work tests (DWP 2012a, 2012b). They will freeze child benefit until 2013 and remove it from the better-off, cut working families tax credit, reduce the social housing budget by three-quarters (IFS 2011, table 6.2) and intro-duce harsher entitlement rules and a series of cuts to housing benefit that will limit entitlement for single and for younger people, make it difficult to claim outside low-income areas and for many kinds of housing and reduce benefit levels sharply. These cuts impact with particular severity on women, who are the main recipients of child benefit, tax credit and housing benefit, and make up some 90 per cent of single parents, and children.

Changes to the benefit uprating rules will result in further reductions in spending on benefits for people of working age that will continue to drive down costs indefinitely. Uprating for pensions will be set at the highest of the retail price index, rises in earnings or 2.5 per cent, ensur-ing that this group shares the improvements in living standards of the mass of the population. Rises in benefits for those of working age (child benefit, housing benefit, job seeker's allowance, income support and tax credits) will be limited to 1 per cent between 2013–14 and 2015–16 and then linked to the Consumer Price Index. This index does not include mortgage interest and calculates below the arithmetic average of prices for the items included on the assumption that purchasers will continually substitute cheaper for more expensive ones. The projected outcome is to reduce the rate at which benefits rise every year by between 1 and 2 per cent indefinitely. Lower-income families of working age will experience harsh immediate cuts in living standards and a continuing downward pressure, which will exacerbate the division between better- and worse-off groups. About two-thirds of the money saved will come from benefits paid to women (WBG 2012b, 3).

The division between welfare for working age poor and for pensioners will be embodied in a re-configuration of the benefit system. All benefits except child benefit and those for pensioners will be combined into a new Universal Credit from 2013. The new system will have the advantages of simplicity and transparency and will mitigate slightly the 'poverty trap', whereby people moving off benefit into paid work may experience only a small increase in net income because they risk losing benefits nearly pound for pound against any extra money they earn. Of the 7.1 million people likely to be claiming the benefit, some 2.9 million working-age families will experience a short-term net gain, against some 1.8 million, mainly single people, who will lose out (IFS 2012c). However the cuts in uprating and other restrictions described above will continue to drive down living standards for the poor. The pressures on benefits will be intensified by further cuts in the 2013 budget of about £1.2bn (Adam 2012). Current proposals will direct the new benefit to the chief earner in the household, typically a male partner in a couple, so that women will tend to lose control over benefit incomes (WBG 2011b). DWP modelling shows that the rates at which benefits are lost if income rises are on average higher for women, so that the incentive to work more is reduced, again leading to outcomes in which women are more dependent on men (DWP 2011a,16).

New policies cut back means-testing for pensioners just as they extend it for those of working age. A new single-tier flat-rate pension will be introduced in 2017 to replace the current National Insurance Basic Pension, some of the means-tested Pension Credit to which those without other sources of income are entitled, and the additional State Second Pension to which those above a minimum income level contribute. The new pension has the advantage of simplicity and is set at a level slightly higher (some two pounds) than the amount all pensioners are entitled to under Pension Credit. It will benefit those on low incomes and self-employed people. It is unclear how many of those with interrupted work records (mainly women) who currently rely on pension credit will gain from the reform. A 35-year contribution record is required to receive full single-tier pension. Those with caring responsibilities will have some contributions credited but an extended work record is required to gain from the new benefit. Those who pay into an additional private or occupational pension and their employers will lose the current relief on NI contributions (DWP 2013, 9–10). The government expects more people to enrol in private top-up pensions as the size of the state pension becomes clearer but these pensions will become more expensive as the subsidy is removed.

The scale of the cutbacks for benefits for sick and disabled people of working age has attracted some surprise. This group typically attracts low levels of stigma since it is not seen as responsible for its inability to work. Policy announcements have stressed the role of work tests in implementing these cuts. Part of the explanation for these cuts may be the sums involved: more than 9 per cent of all benefit spending (Browne and Hood 2012, table 2.1). Part may be the fact that the risk of disability is concentrated among lower social groups, attracting less sympathy from the middle mass. Those in routine and manual work report roughly twice as much limiting long-standing illness or disability as those in professional or managerial jobs (Palmer 2011, Graph 5).

DOI: 10.1057/9781137328113

Figure 1.3 shows the percentage fall in income as a result of the tax and benefit changes for different tenths of the income distribution, from poorest to richest, and for pensioners, households with children and those without. It brings home two points: in general it is a small minority of the richest who are hit the hardest as a result of the tax changes, but those at the bottom also suffer disproportionately because they face severe benefit cuts (HM Treasury 2012a, chart 1b). Second the impact on other groups is very different according to household type. Pensioners mostly are relatively well protected. Among household with children, the bottom three income groups are hit relatively hard. Among those without children, the cuts for those at the bottom are very harsh indeed. This group includes people with low skills and poor work opportunities who are vulnerable to severe poverty. Poverty (understood as income below 60 per cent of the average) will continue to rise, from 19.1 to 20.8 per cent among households with children and from 15.4 to 16.8 per cent among working-age adults by 2015 (Joyce 2012, table 3). Cuts in social services provision affecting health and social care, nurseries, housing and local government services will also impact more heavily on the poor.

The overall local government cutback is 30 per cent over five years, affecting pre-school and 16–19 college education, the careers service,

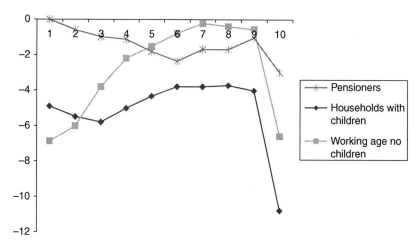

FIGURE 1.3   *The impact of tax and benefit cuts on incomes for different household and income groups 2010 to 2015 (%)*

Source: Calculated from Adam (2012).

DOI: 10.1057/9781137328113

local housing and transport, youth work, public health and most importantly care for frail and older people and for children, and social housing. Councils will differ in how they prioritise spending challenges. We have already noted that the main source of support for social housing, the communities' budget, is cut by three-quarters. The changes to the formula for allocating funding from central to local government, which makes up about three-quarters of local spending, more in poorer, lower community charge areas, visit cuts emphatically on these areas. Support falls by roughly three times as much in inner cities and poorer parts of England than in more affluent rural and suburban districts (IFS 2012b, chapter 6, see also HoC Library 2011, Tables 4 and 5, and PWC 2010, 2–3). These shifts have led to service cuts, mergers of provision by councils and much greater use of outsourcing to private contractors (Johnstone 2011). Whether one-off savings from such changes can be repeated in future years is unclear (Moore 2010). Similar changes have been made to the area component in NHS funding allocations (Bambra 2012).

When the cuts in services are combined with those in benefits and with the tax changes, the full impact is heaviest for poorer people of working age. The effects are particularly severe for families compared with single people. It is difficult to cost the loss of services. Not being able to send a child to a nursery or to get social care provision may have a greater impact on a family's life than is indicated by the cash value of the place. IFS have attempted to parcel out the impact of the cuts in services, assuming these are worth what it costs to provide them and not taking into account the 2013 budget cuts. The estimate shows that services cuts reduce the living standards of the poorest fifth of households by a further 4 per cent and of the better-off fifth by about 2 per cent (Browne 2010, O'Dea 2010).

Cuts that affect poor families have a strong impact on women, since women tend to be lower paid than men and more likely to be unwaged due to caring responsibilities. About 70 per cent of tax credits, including childcare and working tax credits and other support, is paid to mothers, as is 94 per cent of child benefit. Some 60 per cent of housing benefit, also due to be cut, is paid to women (Cooper, 2010, reported in Stratton, 2010). The shift to Universal Credit will further deepen women's dependence on men in families as explained above. The policy of raising income tax thresholds benefits men disproportionately since women predominate among those paid below the minimum tax level (WBG 2012b, 9). An overall analysis by the HoC Library of the combined effect of all income

DOI: 10.1057/9781137328113

tax, tax credit and social security measures from June 2010 to December 2012 shows that 74 per cent of the cuts bear on women's incomes and 26 per cent on men's (Fawcett Society 2012).

Women are also affected differentially by other cuts across the range of government services, since they predominate among lower-income state sector employees, most vulnerable to the impact of central and local government cutbacks and to cost savings in services transferred to the private sector. OBR now estimates that about 1.1 million jobs will be lost in the government sector between 2010 and 2018 (OBR 2012a). Some will be made up in newly privatised services, mostly at lower pay and conditions. About two-thirds of the impact of the cuts to the uprating of public sector pensions (expected to reduce benefit levels by about a fifth by 2030 and ultimately by 40 per cent) will be on women. The cuts affect the poorest groups, especially families, women and children most severely (WBG 2011a).

The cuts will also impact on homelessness. The numbers of households accepted by local authorities in England as homeless and in priority need fell from about 102,000 annually to about 42,000 between 1997 and 2009. It then rose to some 48,000 (June 2012) and continues to rise (DCLG 2012, chart 3, HoC Library 2012, table 1). The long-term context is an established trend to an increase in demand for housing as the number of households rises, from 16.3 million in 1961 to 20.2 in 1981 to 25.3 by 2010 and is predicted to reach 27.5 million by 2033 (ONS 2012a, 1, DCLG 2010). The number of dwellings slightly exceeds that of households, but demand is concentrated, particularly in the Midlands, London and the South-East, producing intense pressure on stock and higher rents and prices in these areas. The problems for low-income and vulnerable groups are exacerbated by the fact that the proportion of all housing provided by social landlords (councils and housing associations) has fallen sharply, from 31 to 20 per cent between 1977 and 2012, as a result of right to buy purchases and limited investment (HoC Library 2012, 2). The cuts in housing benefit mentioned earlier and new rules that allow councils to rehouse vulnerable households in priority need with private landlords without taking the affordability of housing into account are likely to make the problem worse. Some authorities in areas of great housing pressure are moving homeless families outside the borough, often at a considerable distance, in order to find cheap accommodation. This may disrupt family networks, children's schooling and work contacts.

DOI: 10.1057/9781137328113

The risks: The speed and depth of the cutbacks are particularly surprising because they involve major risks in three directions: economically, politically and practically. The economic risk is simply that the assumptions about how government interventions influence the economy may prove incorrect. The decisive shift towards a liberal cutback approach may fail to reduce the deficit or re-establish the conditions for growth. At the time of writing (December 2012) growth is stalled, the deficit expanding and the Office for Budgetary Responsibility assumes it will do so until at least 2017–18 (OBR 2012a, table 1.2). The International Monetary Fund now argues that austerity has had a more damaging effect on economic recovery than was previously assumed and may actually cut growth (IMF 2012, 41). The government is under pressure to regulate the financial sector more strictly and has reluctantly agreed, although serious intervention is postponed until 2019. State-led investment is now being pursued on a modest scale by underwriting bank lending to business and through transport and infrastructure undertakings. These are to be financed through further unspecified cuts to benefits and services from 2013, with the NHS and education largely protected (HM Treasury 2012b).

The political risks are especially serious for a coalition and follow from the economic problems. Continued austerity and failure to achieve key targets in growth and deficit reduction may damage prospects in the 2015 election. The coalition partners, who include some committed to a more centrist agenda, may withdraw support for some agreed policies.

Practical risks concern the policy outcomes. In relation to the welfare state, it seems likely that the government will find it hard to protect those areas it wishes to exempt from cuts. The NHS already faces a strict programme of 4.4 per cent annual savings and is currently achieving about half that level, with much difficulty. Cost pressures are likely to lead to a deterioration in quality of service after 2013 (Appleby *et al.* 2012). IFS estimates that real increases in the cost of staff and other resources in education will raise spending by some 4 per cent by 2015. If extra resources are not found, the effect will be an equivalent spending cut (IFS 2011, table 6.2). The benefit reforms have so far undershot by about one-third the targets for moving substantial numbers from disability benefits or jobseeker's allowance into paid work (DWP 2012e). Further risks are involved in enforcing performance and quality targets on outsourced programmes. We consider why a coalition should chose to run such risks in more detail in Chapter 2 and discuss the problems of regulating risk in Chapter 4.

DOI: 10.1057/9781137328113

Restructuring public services

The UK government leads the way in liberal responses to the economic crisis. It is pursuing a major programme of cutbacks intended to last beyond the life of the current parliament and involving substantial economic, political and practical risks. The cuts have been combined with a thorough-going restructuring of almost every major area of government activity, designed to change the way in which services are delivered and ensure that cutbacks are embedded permanently in future patterns of provision. For the welfare state, the restructuring includes three main elements: the break-up of large national services so that responsibility moves away from central to local government or to non-state mainly commercial providers, much greater diversity in provision between groups and areas in all services, including those that remain national, and a much greater emphasis on strengthening incentives and mobilising people into paid work. The reform programme, involving the simultaneous restructuring of the NHS (NHS and Social Care Act 2012), local government (Localism Act 2011), benefits for those of working age (Welfare Reform Act 2012), the Employment Service, higher education, social housing, pensions and public administration (*Open Government Services*, Cabinet Office 2011), stands out among the recovery packages of the larger Western democracies in scale and ambition (Hay and Wincott 2012, chapter 1, Farnsworth 2011, 258–61, Taylor-Gooby and Stoker 2011, 4).

Fragmenting national services: The Prime Minister has signalled the 'presumption' of 'all public services being open to outside providers' (Cameron 2011). The Open Public Services White Paper sets out the underlying principles: greater choice, decentralisation of provision, competition and the premise that 'wherever possible, public services should be open to a range of providers competing to offer a better service' with fair access and accountability procedures (Cabinet Office 2011, 9). These policies massively extend the system of contracting out services that has been pursued in school and hospital cleaning, catering and ancillary services, local government and elsewhere for the past two decades. Now contracting is to 'any willing provider', in some cases rephrased as 'any qualified provider'. There is a bias towards commercial providers and a relaxation of the responsibility for government to secure a particular range or standard of provision.

The 2012 NHS reforms follow this pattern. The main providers of health services will be local Clinical Commissioning Groups, GP-led

DOI: 10.1057/9781137328113

and involving other health professionals, run as small businesses and managing a devolved £80bn budget within an overall regulatory framework, but with many fewer targets to direct their practice. The reforms place strong emphasis on competition, particularly on price, and ensure that the regulatory body, Monitor, has a duty to oversee the creation of a competitive market. Almost all competition within the health service was previously between NHS providers and for fixed tariff services so that different hospitals competed to provide surgery, clinical tests or routine therapies on the quality of what they could offer rather than cheapness. Experience of competition on price in the US Medicare and Medicaid schemes indicates that it is hard to resist a decline in quality (Gaynor *et al.* 2010, Gaynor and Town 2012, 76–7). The Department for Health plans to let contracts for about a quarter of its budget during 2012 and 2013, mainly to private for-profit providers. This raises major issues in regulating standards, discussed further in Chapter 4.

The future shape of the service is unclear. There are currently moves by commercial providers, including the large multi-national medical insurance firms and European competitors to win contracts from GP-led commissioning panels. The process of transferring community health services mainly to profit-oriented private groups started in mid-2012. One possibility is a more variegated service with different levels and a wider range of provision and priorities between areas. Much will depend on the decisions made by local Clinical Commissioning Groups, who hold the budgets, and the extent to which government is prepared to commit resources to meet the continuing demographic and other pressures.

In education, decentralising school reforms, initiated by the previous government, are now being expanded on a massive scale with no extra funding. The new Academies and Free Schools will be independent from local government control. Private providers are being encouraged to enter the market. Central regulation of teachers' pay, qualifications and conditions of service is being relaxed in the new types of school. While current account school spending has been maintained, spending on other areas of education has been cut sharply. One effect of the relaxation in regulation which allows hard-pressed councils to divert the money to other uses is that funding for the main pre-school programme, Sure Start, has fallen by about half. The national scheme of cash benefits to encourage low-income students to continue schooling and training beyond the minimum school-leaving age of 16 has been abolished and any continuation depends again on local support.

DOI: 10.1057/9781137328113

Government funding for higher education has been cut by 80 per cent with the assumption that increased fees of up to £9000 a year will make up the difference, so that university teaching is financed almost entirely by students. Loans are available but must be repaid. Analysis of official data for the first year (2011–12) shows a 7.4 per cent fall in admissions across the UK compared with 2009–10 (admissions were distorted upwards in 2010–11 by students foregoing a gap year to avoid the higher fees). The fall was 8.8 per cent in England where fees are highest. Conversely, admission rose by 1.0 per cent in Scotland where fees were not increased and by 0.3 per cent in Wales where they were capped at £3456. Applications fell more sharply among women and for less prestigious institutions and shifted towards directly vocational subjects such as law, medicine, business, engineering and computing (Independent Commission on Fees 2012, 5).

The restructuring of the employment service pioneers an approach to the engagement of the for-profit sector with broader implications: payment by results. Under the Work Programme, contractors, who manage unemployed claimers and provide training and work support, receive the bulk of the money only if they meet certain goals. For example, the claimer must enter and hold a job for a minimum period, three to six months. This system is also being introduced in overseas aid and in some areas of community health care, offender management and social care for young people. If successful, it will open up a new approach to public management by monitoring outcomes rather than standards of provision. How far contractual obligations will be enforceable in the event of failure is unclear. The problems of regulation and monitoring highlighted in the discussion of political risks above redouble.

The government has placed considerable emphasis on the role of Third Sector organisations alongside for-profit providers in engaging local communities in a 'Big Society': 'a broad culture of responsibility, mutuality and obligation' (Cameron 2009). The voluntary sector is very much smaller than the state sector, limiting its potential contribution. Activity is concentrated in particular areas, generally the richer parts of the country (Lyon and Sepulveda 2009, Mohan 2011, 7). It focuses on particular needs (chiefly health care and research, schools and youth clubs, religious groupings and overseas aid) and is not necessarily in a position to substitute for cutbacks in support for the poorest (NCVO 2010, vi, 10). In any case much depends on state support. The sector is enormously diverse. The five areas of provision closest to the state

DOI: 10.1057/9781137328113

services which are now being cut back (employment and training, law and advocacy, education, housing and social services) receive more than half their income from local government through contracts which are now also subject to cuts (NCVO 2011). The capacity of the Third Sector to substitute for government is limited, especially in the current context.

Diversity in provision: The cash benefit, NHS and education reforms have passed into law and are now being implemented. Local government cuts, employment service changes and the new rules for pension uprating are established by ministerial decision. It appears certain that the moves towards decentralisation, much greater use of contracts and shifting responsibility away from ministers for outcomes in services like the NHS will lead to greater diversity in provision. In health care, the GP-led Clinical Commissioning Groups will be able to decide on priorities and spend state resources to promote them to a much greater extent than at present. Local state schools constituted as separate semi-autonomous agencies will vary in curriculum, staffing and de facto admission policies. Local government services, especially in social care, will depend very much on variations in local resources.

The combination of cutback and restructuring will impact differently the better- and worse-off, women and men and richer and poorer areas, deepening social divisions. Cash benefits targeted on lower-income people of working age have been cut most sharply while those directed to pensioners have been protected. Reforms to housing benefit will concentrate on poorer households in the lowest rental areas of cities. The impact of changes in local government funding is roughly three times as severe in the most deprived areas as in the least deprived. Some specific grants, such as those for the educational maintenance allowance, Sure Start day nurseries or community charge benefit for poorer payers, have been reduced and authorities given discretion to divert money elsewhere. Local government is prevented by heavy financial penalties from making up the shortfall through higher community charges. The fact that the cuts will hit families of working age and women in those areas more severely has already been discussed.

The decentralisation of provision and outsourcing of major parts of large national services such as the NHS and education will lead to greater spatial divisions as GP-led commissioners or consortia of schools pursue their own policies and make different arrangements with suppliers. One tendency is for the linkages within national services that spread good practice and improved national standards, for example, the cancer and

DOI: 10.1057/9781137328113

heart disease networks in the NHS, to be weakened to enable separate contracting and promote local responsibility. In local government the biggest cutbacks are in office services such as planning and development (43 per cent according to IFS), while social care (the biggest area of council spending) has suffered only a 4 per cent cut nationally. Transport has been cut by about one-fifth and social housing by three-quarters with big local variations (IFS 2012b, chapter 6).

Mobilisation into paid work: The reforms place great emphasis on programmes to move more claimers into paid work. The structural reforms of benefits, in particular the greater emphasis within Universal Credit on weakening the poverty trap, the redefinition of part-time work so that tax credits are no longer available to those working between 16 and 24 hours a week, the determination to shift some two-fifths of those currently claiming disability benefits into the labour market, the imperative in the 'payment by results' system for the Employment Service to get claimers into jobs and the restriction of support for lone parents to those whose youngest child is under five, all tighten the pressures on claimers. The raising of the pension age to 67 for both women and men by the late 2020s creates a new pool of potential workers.

Lying behind this is an ideological valuing of 'strivers' (Osborne 2012) and 'hard-working families' against the feckless and undeserving poor, presumed to enjoy idleness on benefits. This ignores the fact that most poor people earn their poverty. Fifty-nine per cent of working-age households in poverty after housing costs have at least one adult in full-time work (DWP 2012c, table 5.4db). The welfare state for those of working age is becoming even more work-centred. This draws a sharp distinction between those within and outside the realm of employment and maps it onto a corresponding division between deserving and undeserving poor.

The long-run crisis

The headlong cuts and root and branch restructuring of the welfare state are the government's response to the immediate crisis of public spending. This approach is an extreme outlier in the international context, driven by commitment to a radical liberal political economy. The current crisis is set in the context of longer-run pressures which escalate costs in the higher spending areas of social provision and call the future

DOI: 10.1057/9781137328113

stability of the state welfare system into question. The main pressures are as follows:

▸ Population ageing, with increases in the numbers claiming pensions and using health services and social care, which will far outweigh a projected decline in numbers in education;

▸ Continuing pressures for wage rises in these services to match those in the rest of the economy although productivity does not rise at the same rate; and

▸ Social factors such as shifts in expectations about service standards and changes in family support which are substantial but often hard to quantify.

We will examine the three areas: population ageing, the impact of sluggish productivity in welfare services on costs and the social context.

Population ageing and rising demand for health, social care and pensions: People tend to live longer lives, have fewer children and have them rather later in life. As a result the average age of UK citizens will rise as time goes on, an effect amplified by the post-war demographic bulge. The proportion of the population over 65 is expected to increase from 17 to roughly 26 per cent between 2012 and 2061 (OBR 2012c, para 22). Population structures are also affected by other factors such as the mortality of children and young people, which is gradually falling, and immigration, which has made a marked contribution in recent years, but is expected to continue at a substantial but rather lower rate. Population ageing and falling mortality apply across most European countries. The UK is expected to age rather more gradually than many, mainly because immigration will bring in extra people of working age. The projected population increase is from 62 million in 2010 to about 79 million by 2060, slightly ahead of France, rising from 65 to 74 million. Italy will grow from 60 to 65 and Spain from 46 to 52 million. On the other hand, the population of Germany, where population ageing is further advanced and expected immigration lower, will fall from about 82 to 66 million (EC 2012, 26).

Changes in population structure affect public spending. Pensions, of course, apply to older people. The distribution of health care spending by age peaks for those over 65, at about £15,000 a year on average, and for those aged five or younger, at about £5000 a year. Spending on those in between is on average lower. Social care spending hits a peak in advanced old age (£6000 a year for those aged 85 or over) and education

DOI: 10.1057/9781137328113

among the young, averaging £12,000 a year at age 12. Aggregate social spending is relatively high for young people, averaging about £18,000 a year for those aged 10 to 12, lower at about £8000 a year in middle age, then rises steadily from age 65 to plateau at age 85 at about £27,000 a year. The distribution of tax payments is much flatter, with a peak at about age 45 (OBR 2012c, 65). Population ageing increases demand but doesn't increase revenue.

As the population ages, spending will increase, from 36 per cent of GDP in 2016–17 to 41 per cent by 2061–2, according to the OBR projections. Rising health spending is the main factor, followed by pension and social care costs. The estimates refer to an extended time period and do not allow for any changes in unemployment or the possibility that productivity will fall as population ageing slows enterprise and innovation (estimated by the EC to cut EU growth rates from 1.6 to 1.3 per cent annually after 2030: EC 2012, 32). They are highly sensitive to fluctuations, for example in the cost of health care or in immigration rates. However, projections by the EC point to broadly similar increases and show that the UK is slightly below the European average and clearly below Germany, Spain and Italy in the impact of ageing on public finances. The precise impact of the changes is uncertain but likely to be significant and expansionary. It will be very much greater if the kinds of efficiency gains in welfare state services discussed below cannot be achieved.

Productivity and staff costs: The main welfare state services, health and social care and education, employ large and increasing numbers of people. Numbers employed in education rose from 1.4 to 1.6 million and in the NHS from 1.2 to 1.6 million between 1999 and 2011 (ONS 2012b). Pay constitutes the major part of the costs of running these services. Under normal conditions, the economy grows and produces more each year. Part of the extra product is allocated in pay increases for workers in the private sector. Staff in the welfare state sector will expect pay rises at roughly the same rate, although their contribution to the economy is indirect in enabling the private sector to generate a greater surplus.

Productivity in welfare state services is typically understood as the relationship between the output of the service (such factors as numbers of patients treated or students taught) and the input (the money and other resources spent), taking account of any changes in quality (measured by factors such as patient satisfaction, waiting times or examination passes). In education and health care the main input is staff pay. Workers in these

DOI: 10.1057/9781137328113

sectors are likely to demand the same wage increases as elsewhere in the economy, where rises reflect greater productivity and economic growth. The problem is that it is very difficult to achieve real increases in the output of these services year by year comparable to those in the economy as a whole. In many areas, real gains can be achieved by automation, use of ICT and new management techniques. The human services are intricate operations, and often it is the time spent in contact with skilled (and expensive) professionals that people value most highly and that seems to produce the results. It is difficult, for example, for every teacher to teach larger classes year on year or for a surgeon to do more hip replacements.

Enormous efforts have been spent on trying to achieve real improvements in welfare state productivity in recent years. These have included: introducing competition between the various clinics, schools and other agencies within state services or between state and non-state, commercial on not-for-profit providers in education and NHS front-line services from the early 1990s onwards; a number of experiments with ICT, including the ambitious attempt to establish a national system of access to patients records between 2005 and 2011 only partially successful; 'efficiency saving' cost-paring measures from the mid-1980s onwards; a target-centred management system through Public Service Agreements developed from the 1998 Comprehensive Spending Review onwards, radically scaled back in 2010; the 'Nicholson Challenge' from 2009, intended to produce 4 per cent savings annually in the NHS from 2009 onwards, succeeding at less than half that rate; pay freezes, which damage recruitment if maintained; and now payment by results.

It is difficult to estimate productivity for services like the NHS and education because the quality of provision is often a matter of judgement. The most recent ONS estimates take into account measures of output (patients treated, students in schools) and also of quality (waiting times, patient satisfaction survey results, the success of treatment, exam pass rates, test results, school satisfaction and similar factors). They conclude that overall output in health and social care kept pace with inputs between 1995 and 2001. Resources for health care increased sharply after 2001 but had little immediate effect on output, so productivity actually fell between 2001 and 2004. From 2005 to 2009 productivity has been largely unchanged. The net effect over the whole 14 years is a slight average annual fall (−0.2 per cent: Hardie *et al.* 2011). For education, productivity grew in the early period as the school age population expanded, fell in the middle period as this was outstripped by extra funding, then

DOI: 10.1057/9781137328113

increased after 2004 as funding increments tailed off and quality measured by exam results rose. Overall, productivity declined, but at an even slower rate than in the case of health (Baird *et al.* 2010).

Attempts to examine a longer period run into further data problems. Research by the University of York shows a broadly similar pattern, while work that attempts to look back to 1979–80 suggests a gradual productivity improvement under more stable financing (Oliver 2005). Le Grand's summary of recent evidence implies that some, at least, of the quality improvement is due to greater competition between health service providers (2007). It is unclear whether productivity in the private sector is greater or lower than in the public sector (Jurd 2011), and how far gains from privatisation result from changes such as a shift to non-unionised labour that cannot be repeated over time.

The overall picture is inconclusive but carries a strong suggestion that productivity improvements in the main welfare state services are much harder to achieve than in the private non-welfare sector, where annual productivity rises are normal and average just over 2 per cent a year for the whole period between 1990 and 2011, including the first recession (OECD 2012a). This matters: if the state sector does not make productivity gains at the same rate as the private sector but wants similar pay rises it must find ways to reduce costs or spend more money each year. By way of illustration, the Office for Budgetary Responsibility in its projections estimates the impact on health care costs of differences in productivity. If productivity in health care matches that in the rest of the economy, overall costs will grow steadily from about 6 per cent of GDP in 2016–17 to about 9 per cent by 2061–2, mainly as a result of demographic shifts. This is a real but manageable pressure. If productivity fails to improve, costs inch up to 10 per cent of GDP by 2031–2, nearly 15 per cent by 2041–2 and to 24 per cent by the end of the period (OBR 2012c, chart b5). To shift from 6 per cent of GDP to nearly 25 per cent on health care would have major consequences for the rest of social spending and for the economy as a whole. However, experience indicates that the most stringent efforts can do little more than hold productivity constant.

Social changes: family structure, standards and expectations: Some of the other factors likely to influence public spending are also difficult to quantify. These include: changes in family structure, which will probably increase the proportion of people in paid work but also affect demand for accommodation and reduce the amount of informal family care available,

DOI: 10.1057/9781137328113

and the demands that people make for higher standards in public services as they become increasingly aware of what is technically available or is provided elsewhere.

Family structure: The rising pressure on housing as the number of households increases has already been discussed. At the same time gender roles are changing. The numbers of women in work and the numbers who combine work with childcare have risen steadily. The proportion of men in paid work fell from 95 to 83 per cent between 1971 and 2011, while that of women rose from 56 to 70 per cent. Seventy-one per cent of mothers with dependent children were in paid work by 2011, up from 66 per cent in 1996, against 90 per cent of fathers in both years (ONS 2012c). Current benefit reforms will withdraw benefits from mothers of school age children, increasing work incentives for this group at the same time as cuts to childcare support and other services make it more difficult for mothers to pursue employment.

Standards in public services: This raises complex issues. Society has become more individualistic, people are typically better educated, feel that a greater range of opportunities should be open to them and are generally less deferential and more confident in their own judgements (Giddens 1995, chapter 4). One result is a much greater awareness of attainable standards in such services as health care and education and a willingness to demand better provision. Two outcomes can be identified. First people experience treatment as consumers rather than clients in the private sector and increasingly expect the same when they use state services (Glennerster 2010). One result has been a move towards user choice in health and social care services and towards much greater personalisation in provision (see Chapter 4). This has encouraged the development of personal budgeting where health and social care services may make available (within constraints) the relevant budget to individual users, who then decides how to spend the money to best meet their own needs (Glendinning *et al.* 2009). If resources are constrained, users may end up supplementing payments from their own purse.

Another development is much greater willingness for service users to pursue litigation to demand higher quality treatment or to protest against apparent shortfalls. The total cost of NHS compensation claims has risen from £550 million in 2001–2 to £1329 million in 2011–12 (NHS Litigation Authority 2012). A series of demands from suppliers and patients for new and expensive treatments to be funded by the NHS exerts significant pressures on the drugs bill.

DOI: 10.1057/9781137328113

All these changes alter the environment in which the welfare state operates and increase pressure for radical changes, in most cases increasing the cost of maintaining provision. The profound and immediate cuts and restructuring currently underway are set in the context of a longer-run crisis resulting from established trends towards rising real costs for the most expensive areas of social provision, an increase in the proportion of older people in the population and social and attitudinal changes that are likely to escalate demands. These demands bear mainly but not exclusively on the mass services that make up the bulk of current spending. It is because the cutbacks are set in this context that the pressures on public provision are so intense and bear so heavily on the least popular areas of provision, for the poorest groups.

Conclusions

This chapter makes three points:

▸ The UK welfare state faces an immediate crisis as resources are cut back precipitately and services are restructured, fragmented and privatised. These policies carry real political, economic and practical risks. They may damage support as voters lose valued services, they may fail to restore growth, as investment is reduced, and they may fail to deliver services of acceptable standard. For political reasons the cuts are imposed most stringently on welfare for lower-income minorities of working age, impacting most severely on women and children among them. Health care, pensions and education, the welfare state services most valued by the mass of the population, escape the harshest cuts, but still face real pressures. The current government is addressing the immediate crisis in a way that deepens divisions between the mass and the more vulnerable poorer minorities.

▸ These changes are taking place in the context of long-run pressures from population ageing, continuing wage escalation and other factors, which bear mainly on the popular services, predominantly on health and social care and pensions. More resources are required over time simply to maintain standards. Demands for extra spending here intensify the squeeze on benefits for the poor of working age since the mass services are more highly valued

DOI: 10.1057/9781137328113

by most voters. The long-run crisis becomes a continuing war of attrition to slow the rise in costs for these services.

▶ These issues are important across almost all developed countries. They are particularly intransigent in the UK, because the government has decided to respond to the immediate crisis through cutbacks rather than investment, because it imposes the cuts most stringently on vulnerable lower-income groups, because a liberal ideology intensifies the divisions between deserving and undeserving groups and because the impact of global trends to greater inequality and social division is particularly marked in this country.

The next chapter steps back from cutbacks and restructuring and analyses the broader social and political context in which these changes are taking place. It considers why government chooses to respond to the immediate crisis in the way that it has despite the economic, political and practical risks outlined above, and shows that an underlying project to entrench a radical, competitive and individualistic liberalism permanently in the UK political economy is at least part of the explanation.

DOI: 10.1057/9781137328113

2
Why Add Restructuring to Cutbacks? Explaining the New Policy Direction

Abstract: *The new policies involve real political, social and economic risks. One explanation rests on short-term party-political considerations, another on an economics that prioritises deficit reduction against any other goal. Neither is convincing. Britain has moved from a European to a US pattern of social inequalities during the past 30 years, due to changes in work, in patterns of residence and in the overall power of capital against labour. These shifts combine with currents in public opinion and in mass politics that strengthen social divisions and erode support for inclusive welfare. They provide the opportunity for government to move decisively against the welfare state tradition and to entrench a radical, competitive and individualistic liberalism permanently in the national political economy.*

Keywords: cuts; inequality; liberalism poverty; risks; segmentation; social divisions

Taylor-Gooby, Peter. *The Double Crisis of the Welfare State and What We Can Do About It.* Basingstoke: Palgrave Macmillan, 2013. DOI: 10.1057/9781137328113

DOI: 10.1057/9781137328113

In this chapter we analyze the broader context in which political struggles over the future of the welfare state are taking place and consider why a coalition government under difficult economic circumstances should take the risks involved in combining rapid cuts with a root-and-branch restructuring of virtually the entire public sector.

The chapter falls into two sections. The first sets the longer-term context: on the one hand, higher incomes and better living standards, on the other growing inequalities, deepening divisions between better- and worse-off groups and harsher stigmatisation for claimers of working age. The second argues that the scale and riskiness of the new programme can be explained only through a commitment to entrench a new radical liberalism in British public life.

At the practical level, the cutbacks can be seen as intended to gain support from those who resent welfare state dependency, to save resources and facilitate tax cuts, and to ensure financial stability and make Britain attractive to overseas investors. Current policies do not appear successful by any of these criteria. Further explanations analyse the new policies from the perspective of political economy. From this viewpoint, they form part of a broader project designed to tackle the problem of Britain's long-run economic decline from a particular perspective. Although growth continues in the UK, other capitalist economies have gradually outstripped it during the post-war period. The emergence of new global players in Asia and South America pushes Britain further back into the second division.

Cutbacks plus restructuring are intended to entrench a permanent liberalism by undermining the social solidarity that sustained the welfare state, creating new pro-market lobbies and shifting the political climate in a direction more supportive of a competitive, market-centred social order. This is a particular solution to the problem of finding a way forward for the British economy in a post-industrialised and globalised world. It ignores alternatives in which state welfare plays a much stronger role.

The context: growth and inequality

Growing income inequalities: Economic growth during most of the post-war period has led to higher living standards and the rise of a mass consumption society. During the period up to the mid-1970s incomes rose at roughly the same rate for most population groups and rather

DOI: 10.1057/9781137328113

more slowly for those at the top, so that the gap narrowed slightly. Subsequently, top incomes have grown much faster and those at the bottom have fallen behind.

This pattern may be summarised in terms of three overall trends, presented in Figures 2.1, 2.2 and 2.3:

▸ For the mass of the population, incomes roughly doubled in real terms between the early 1960s and 2010. Economic inequalities have tended to 'fan out' as relatively higher-income and lower-income groups move away from the median, the better-off more rapidly than those on more modest incomes. The bottom tenth were about £90 (in 2010–11 equivalent monetary amounts prices) below the median in 1961 and just over £205 below in 2010. Correspondingly the top tenth were about £150 above and are now about £440 above. Inequality accelerated from the mid-1980s onwards (Figure 2.1).

▸ For a small minority at the very top (the top one or 0.1 per cent) incomes have grown very much more rapidly than for the mass of the population: the available statistics indicate that the top 10 per cent have increased their share of total incomes by a quarter

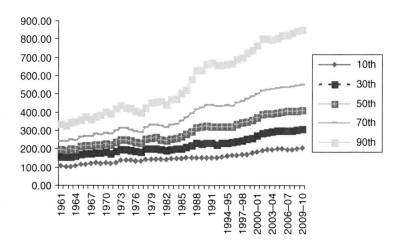

FIGURE 2.1   *Income inequality for the mass of the population, 1961–2010*

Note: Household income net of direct taxes and including state benefits, expressed as equivalent monetary amounts for a typical childless couple (£ per week before housing costs); GB, FES to 1993–4, then FRS.

Source: IFS.

DOI: 10.1057/9781137328113

and the top 5 per cent by a half, while the top 0.1 per cent have improved theirs by a factor of three (Figure 2.2). The figures refer only to incomes known to revenue authorities and are almost certainly an underestimate.

▸ For those at the very bottom, poverty shows a different pattern, initially stabilising, then rising rapidly in the mid and late 1980s. This was followed again by stability and then a slight fall in the early 2000s, resulting from high employment coupled with the introduction of the minimum wage and tax credits. The numbers in poverty rose from 2006 to 2007 and declined slightly after 2009 as wages fell faster than benefits (Figure 2.3).

Inequalities in wealth also appear to have grown, although information is again limited by what is declared to HMRC. Personal wealth declared for tax purposes roughly doubled from 4 to 8 per cent of incomes between 1977 and 2005. The holdings of the richest increased much faster. Dorling and others estimate that the percentage of 'exclusively wealthy' households (who use only private schools and health care and own more than two properties and other high value items such as boats) rose from 3.5 to 5.6 per cent between 1990 and 2000, while the proportion of poor households grew from 21.3 to 27 per cent (Dorling and Ballas 2008, 127).

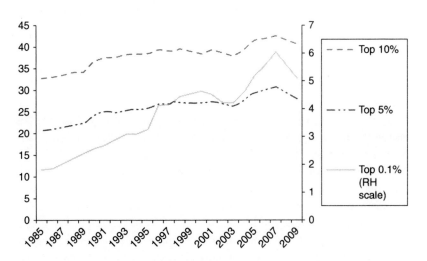

FIGURE 2.2   *Top incomes as percentage of total incomes, 1985–2010*
Source: Alvaredo *et al.* (2012).

DOI: 10.1057/9781137328113

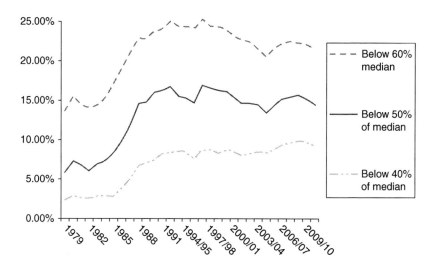

FIGURE 2.3   *Percentage in poverty after housing costs, 1979–2011*
Source: IFS.

Wealthy and poor households have become increasingly segregated in where they live and work, so that growing inequalities in income and wealth lead to deeper divisions between social groups.

Inequality has grown more rapidly in the UK than elsewhere in Europe, but slightly more slowly than that in the US. Figure 2.4 shows trends in Gini coefficients, a widely used overall measure of inequality, designed so that 1 equals hypothetical perfect inequality, with all resources in the hands of one household, and 0 perfect equality. In the mid-1970s household incomes (before taxes and transfer payments) in the UK were rather more equal than in the US, Canada and Sweden and on a par with Japan. The UK became rapidly more unequal during the late 1970s and early 1980s and overtook Canada, Sweden and Germany by 1990, and then the US and France in the late 1990s. More recently inequality has reached a plateau rather below levels in Italy, the most unequal of the major capitalist economies, and at levels close to those in Germany. The operation of taxes and benefits mitigates inequality everywhere. After taxes and benefits the UK is in fact a more unequal society than any other G7 nation apart from the US and on a par with Italy (US 0.38, UK 0.34, Italy 0.34, Japan 0.33 Canada 0.32, Germany 0.30 and France 0.29). In social inequality, as in public spending, the UK is becoming less like a European and more like a transatlantic nation. The

DOI: 10.1057/9781137328113

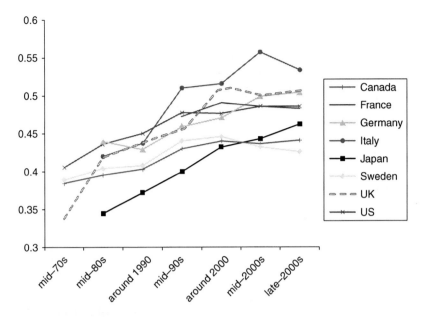

FIGURE 2.4 *Inequality, G7 countries and Sweden, mid-1970s to 2010 (before taxes and transfers)*

Source: OECD (2012a).

programme of cutbacks focused on the poor will exacerbate inequality and push the UK even closer to the US.

The trend to greater economic inequality appears to be driven by three factors:

▸ The opening up of global markets that expose more people to stricter competitive pressures, coupled with technical changes in production that put a higher premium on skill and reduce the number of un- and semi-skilled jobs, amplifies the return to education, training and skill level. Those with less to offer are relatively more disadvantaged in a larger market, while those with scarce abilities can command a greater reward (Green 2013);

▸ Changes in the organisation of work as the labour market in developed economies moves from factory-based manufacturing to more fragmented service sector work directly affects inequalities. Manufacturing economies provide a range of skilled and semi-skilled jobs which pay adequate wages. The distribution of pay in service sector work spans a much

DOI: 10.1057/9781137328113

broader range from low-paid (retail, personal care, call-centre) to high-skilled (financial, legal, education and health service) work. It also weakens the capacity of labour to organise and strengthens capital. One outcome is the tendency since the late 1970s for an increasing proportion of the value added in national economies each year to go to capital and a smaller proportion to employees (Bailey *et al.* 2011, Glynn 2006). Another is the trend to intensification of work (Green 2006).

▸ The impact of these changes is amplified by political developments: on the one hand the weakening of trade unions is reflected in stricter legal restrictions on mobilisation and industrial action from the 1980s onwards. On the other, advantaged groups are in a better position to press home their advantage. The norms that govern remuneration at the top end become less influenced by ideas about the accepted ratio between return to a manager and those she manages and more by a market logic in which the ceiling is the highest comparable pay globally (Atkinson 2008). Increasingly wealthy minorities are able to exert more power over distribution and tax policies and gear up inequalities (Hacker and Pierson 2010). One issue is that small groups in areas such as finance are able to extract extra returns as 'rents' by virtue of their crucial position in the system (Stiglitz 2012).

In addition, population ageing reinforces the lifetime component in wealth inequalities. The trend for women to move into full-time work and for people to marry others in the same income group compounds the effect of labour market inequalities. Lower tax rates on capital and at the top end as governments seek to attract investment and skilled labour in a more globalised world weaken restraints on inequality. All these factors generate greater inequalities in market incomes and make the task for a government that wishes to reduce inequality harder. They also set in train self-gearing processes. Those already advantaged are, because of their advantage, better able to perpetuate and to widen inequalities. As organised political groups they lobby for their own interests. As individuals they are better able to ensure their families have the best access to education, training and opportunities.

These factors operate with particular force in the UK. The shift away from a manufacturing to a service sector economy has moved more rapidly here than among the other main European countries. In the UK 82 per cent of the workforce worked in the service sector as against

76 per cent in France and 74 per cent in Germany, the same proportion as in the US (OECD 2009b). Median wages in the UK grew by about 1 per cent a year between the mid-1990s and the onset of the recession, while GDP grew by nearly 2.5 per cent, with most of the difference going to capital. In the Nordic countries pay kept pace with growth, in Germany it did so up to about 2005 and in France up to 2000 (Bailey *et al.* 2011, 35–7). Differences in educational performance are slightly higher than the average across OECD countries by about 2 per cent. The striking finding from the PISA international comparison is that in 2009 socio-economic factors accounted for 77 per cent of the difference in performance, against an average of 55 per cent. The UK family background component is higher than in any of the 36 developed countries included, apart from Luxembourg (OECD 2009a, 1). The UK has the weakest employment protection and the largest financial sector among major European countries (OECD 2012a).

In addition the institutional structure of the British welfare state is less well-fitted to command mass loyalty. The national insurance system established after the Second World War produced lower benefits and a weaker sense of entitlement than did social insurance in France and Germany. The 2013 reforms almost completely abolish insurance rights to benefits for low-income people. Contributions will still be levied. These form a much smaller proportion of welfare state finance than elsewhere (6.7 per cent in the UK, 16.8 in France and 14.3 in Germany: OECD 2012a). A much greater share of social security finance comes from employers in France and Germany (11.3 and 6.7 per cent) than in the UK (3.8 per cent), pointing to a weakness in the capacity to generate revenue.

The 2007–8 crisis produced a real fall in GDP of more than 5 per cent, of which about half had been made up by June 2012 (Figure 1.1). Current OBR projections indicate that the rest will not be recouped until at least 2017–18 and probably later (OBR 2012a). IFS estimate that this will translate into a 7.1 per cent fall in net household incomes at the median between 2009–10 and 2014–15, with a slight narrowing for the mass, a fall in benefit incomes for unemployed families, disabled people and single parents, and an increase in the number of children in poverty of at least 400,000. Wages failed to keep pace with prices in 2010–11, but benefits were uprated by price indices so that they in fact outstripped earnings, and the poverty statistic fell. This effect will be abruptly reversed as reforms cut the rate at which benefits can rise to 1 per cent from 2013 to

DOI: 10.1057/9781137328113

2016 and target them more strictly. The impact of recession at the very top is unclear. The first two at least of the long-term drivers of inequality mentioned above will continue and the underlying factors which drive the trends to greater inequality and higher poverty persist.

Unemployment remained relatively low during the period of growth in the 1950s and 1960s, rising in the crises of the late 1960s and mid-1970s and to a peak of 13 per cent in 1983. It then fell to about 7 per cent by 1990, rose in the 1993 crisis to over 10 per cent and declined gradually to below 5 per cent by 2005. It accelerated during the 2007–8 crisis to exceed 8 per cent by 2010. It is not expected to fall below this level until 2014–15 at the very earliest. Many commentators believe current levels do not yet reflect the full severity of the recessions. The proportion of the labour force unable to find full-time work and involuntarily working part-time more than doubled from 8 per cent in September 2005 to 18 per cent by June 2012 (Grice 2012, chart 5, ONS 2008, 2012).

Social divisions and segregation: The evidence of Dorling and others indicates that the divisions between poorer and richer areas are becoming more marked. These operate at the regional level between North and South and more locally between desired and less attractive areas of cities. Spatial divisions have always been important. These grow deeper as income inequalities widen and people are able to travel longer distances to work. Economic activity has become more concentrated in London and the South-East. Gross value added (an overall measure of the value of goods and services produced) per head rose by 10 per cent in London and 4 per cent in the South-East between 1992 and 2009, but fell by 7 per cent in the North-East and 5 per cent in the North-West. Average household incomes in the North-East stood at 71 per cent of those in London in 1997 but had fallen to 66 per cent by 2009. For the North-West corresponding statistics are 75 and 70 per cent (ONS 2011, Tables 3.3 and 3.4). At the more local level, factors such as quality of housing, air pollution, transport links and quality of schools play a part. Current policies which restrict those on housing benefits to the poorer areas of cities and impose the most severe cuts on central allocations to local authorities and the NHS in deprived areas can only aggravate these trends.

Inequality and stigma: Inequality matters because greater inequality and social segregation diminish sympathy between social groups. At the same time, greater social distance implies that poverty or low living standards elsewhere are less likely to visit demands for more welfare or problems of urban disorder on those who are comfortably off. Both

DOI: 10.1057/9781137328113

factors erode willingness to pay the extra taxes necessary to maintain and develop the benefits and services needed for a more redistributive welfare state.

The distinction between deserving and undeserving poor is growing stronger in the popular imagination. Stigma erodes support for collective and generous welfare. Research on attitudes to poverty has generally found a close relationship between the extent to which most people are inclined to view claimers as work-shy scroungers and the economic cycle. Unsurprisingly, when there is stable growth and jobs appear plentiful, stigma increases. When there is an economic downturn and times are tough, it falls. Unemployment peaked in 1983 and later in 1991. The numbers of respondents to the British Social Attitudes survey who took the generous view that benefits 'are too low and cause hardship' exceeded those who claimed they are 'too high and discourage work' in those years. As unemployment fell in the later 1990s and 2000s support for the poor also declined. From the 2007 recession onwards, unemployment rose from 5 per cent in 2005 to 8 per cent by 2010, and the number forced to work part-time doubled. The striking thing is that attitudes to claimers do not become more generous. The punitive view reaches its highest level since 1983 (61 per cent of those interviewed) while the more generous view sinks to its lowest level (22 per cent).

The evidence of escalating benefit stigma is reinforced by analysis of newspaper treatment of those without work (where references to unemployed people as scroungers doubled from 200 to 400 a year in broadsheets between 2003 and 2009) and by the fact that popular support for higher spending on the poor among those interviewed in the annual British Social Attitudes survey halved from just over 60 to 30 per cent between 1987 and 2011 (Taylor-Gooby 2013). Official news-releases and political campaigning by the right representing claimers as work-shy have reinforced perceptions of those on benefits as out of work, fraudulent or irresponsible rather than low-paid or unable to find jobs (Baumberg *et al.* 2012, 48–50).

Taken together these findings indicate a hardening of attitudes against the poor and a shift that reinforces the new individualism. Inequalities have widened and appear likely to continue to do so. Those at the bottom can no longer afford anything close to what those above them consume. The role of the welfare state in their lives becomes more and more important. Longer-term trends to a shrinking manufacturing base, weaker unions, more powerful employers and inequality in access to

DOI: 10.1057/9781137328113

education and training are reinforced by growing social divisions that undermine sympathy between the middle mass and the poor and erode public support for an inclusive welfare state.

Understanding the new directions in policy

First there are practical issues. One way of understanding the new policy directions is that current approaches are popular and will help the government win votes. Another is that the restructuring will save resources and contribute to deficit reduction: cutbacks and restructuring are complementary. A third is that it will contribute directly to economic goals by demonstrating to overseas capital that Britain is determined to preserve economic stability and remains a safe location for investment. These accounts have some strength, but it is not clear that they provide a compelling explanation of why a coalition government under difficult economic circumstances should embark on an uncertain restructuring of almost all of the public sector. For this we need to consider explanations at the level of political economy: the desire to shift the UK economy onto a new course to ensure continued growth and profitability in a highly competitive world, and the possibility that restructuring is designed to embed the new model of the relationship between state and citizen permanently. Most new policy directions are reversed by subsequent governments. Cuts plus restructuring form part of a project to undermine the political ideas and values supportive of an inclusive welfare state and impose an uncompromising liberalism as the future direction of British society.

Practical explanations: politics as usual: The pattern of cutbacks and restructuring clearly advantages some social groups. Voting and opinion poll data indicate some recognition of this. In the 2010 election the main differences in party platforms were on approaches to the economic crisis with immigration policy and confidence in the leader also playing a role. The Ipsos-Mori exit poll (2010) shows that among professional and managerial (AB) voters the Conservative lead over Labour was 17 per cent (up 8 per cent from 2005), for C1 (routine middle class) it was 12 per cent (up 7 per cent). Labour retained its lead among working class voters, but for the skilled working class it fell from 23 per cent in 2005 to 14 per cent. Among unskilled workers the decline was from 15 to 13 per cent. The Conservative lead increased sharply among the middle class,

DOI: 10.1057/9781137328113

but Labour's traditional advantage among skilled workers in relatively stable jobs grew weaker.

In the context of rising inequality and the growth of stigma and social division, voting patterns might help support a micro-political explanation of why government should pursue cutbacks and restructuring. From this perspective, centre and right parties are simply exploiting the widening gap between mass and minority. However, since 2010, public opinion has shifted against cutbacks as incomes are outstripped by inflation and the economy stagnates. The proportion of those interviewed by YouGov in June 2010 at the time of the Emergency Budget who described the policy of cutting spending to reduce the deficit as 'good' was 53 per cent, against 28 per cent thinking it 'bad'. By September 2012 the proportions had almost exactly reversed to 29 versus 53 per cent (YouGov 2012). Views on the fairness with which cuts are managed have also reversed, from 55 per cent against 34 per cent to 22 against 64 per cent.

The authoritative British Social Attitudes survey shows that health care and education have consistently headed the list of priorities for extra government spending since 1983 when the survey began, under nine governments with very different approaches to tax and spending. This priority is shared across the population. However, Ipsos-Mori polling shows that attitudes to welfare benefits for the poor are clearly divided by social group: in September 2012 the Conservatives led by 11 per cent over Labour among ABs as the best party on welfare benefits, but trailed by 18 per cent among DEs. Cuts in welfare for those on low incomes remains one of the few areas where Coalition policies gain overall support. Eighty-four of those questioned in September 2011 wanted to see stricter testing for incapacity benefits (10 per cent do not); 78 against 16 per cent thought job seekers should lose some of their benefits if they refused work; 62 against 27 per cent wanted to see benefits capped for people who have 'too many children'; and 57 against 29 per cent thought those on housing benefit who live in expensive areas should be forced to move (Ipsos-Mori 2011). Given the pattern of public opinion, it is hardly surprising that the current government loads cutbacks differentially onto welfare for stigmatised minorities and away from front-line highly valued mass provision.

The ideology of low taxes, state cutbacks and promotion of the market has been a strong theme in Conservative policies since the New Right shift under Mrs Thatcher in 1979. The Liberal Democrat coalition partners have moved towards market liberalism, as set out in the liberal-leaning

DOI: 10.1057/9781137328113

Orange Book programme in 2004 (Laws and Marshall 2004). A programme which opens up large welfare state markets (some £80bn in the NHS, perhaps £25bn in education, social care and other local government services, £12bn in the Employment Service and up to £5bn in universities) to business groups is also likely to attract support from powerful interests. The cuts are allocated in a way that is least likely to damage those who have traditionally supported the party. Together with restructuring they fit the party's ideology, are targeted in a way that is endorsed by the dominant strand in public opinion and will gain extra support from the new interests that become entrenched in welfare provision.

Practical explanations: restructuring complements cuts by saving money: The contribution of restructuring to cash savings is unclear, since there are immediate expenses to weigh against possible future reductions. Official estimates put the cost of NHS reform at £1.7bn. Others suggest £3bn (HC Health Committee 2010, para 92; Walshe 2010). The Universal Credit reforms are costed at £3bn by OBR (2011b, 65) and the student loan system assumes some 30 per cent of loans written off, about £2bn at current prices (OBR 2011b, 70). The initial cost of benefits under the new Universal Credit programme will exceed of that of the current system by over £1bn in the first three years. It is the separate programme of cutbacks in this area, most importantly the reduction of the rate at which benefits are uprated, that generates savings. It is unclear whether the new system will produce longer-term savings by shifting more claimers into jobs through the largely privatised Work Programme.

The cost savings from outsourcing and privatisation in the health service, education and local government depend on driving down costs through contract and competition. There is considerable experience of cost-saving, particularly in areas where objectives are clearly defined and relatively simple and the incentives and measures of success are transparent (Wilson 2010). This is responsible for the rapid introduction of competitive market systems in many developed countries (OECD 2011b). Whether a programme as wide-ranging and hurried as that currently underway will succeed in regulating providers so that costs are contained without damaging service quality is less clear. Funding problems may undermine political support for the new programme. The evidence on competition, outsourcing and regulation is discussed in more detail in Chapter 4.

Practical explanations: a stable haven for investors? The new liberalism has failed in its immediate objectives of containing the budget deficit and seems unlikely to achieve this within the current parliament. A further argument for cutbacks is that economic strictness enhances the confidence of overseas investors. Coupled with deregulation, lower taxes and a loosely regulated labour market it would attract investment. Figure 2.5 charts trends in foreign investment inflows since 2007, for the US, the EU, the large competitor economies of France and Germany and the UK. At the beginning of the period the UK's economic openness is clearly attractive. It draws in nearly as much investment as the much larger US and about twice as much as Germany and France. As the 2008–9 recession bites, investor confidence collapses everywhere. However in the recovery after 2009, investment in the UK continues to decline but begins to improve in the continental competitors, the EU as a whole and the US. By 2011, investment in the UK has sunk to the level of France and Germany, while the US and the EU draw away. The strategy of economic regeneration has so far failed to attain its objectives.

The arguments considered here explain why adding restructuring to cuts might have seemed attractive to the Coalition at the time of the election. The disappointing outcomes make it hard to understand why the government persists with the programme. The new approach has lost its glamour for voters. While it may produce eventual savings, restructuring

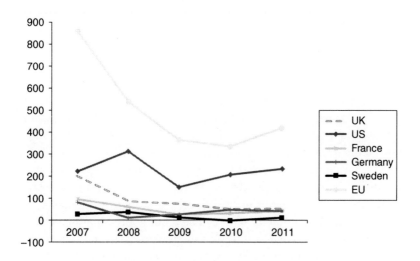

FIGURE 2.5   *Foreign direct investment, selected countries and the EU, 2007–11 ($bn)*
Source: OECD (2012b).

DOI: 10.1057/9781137328113

involves extra short-term spending for uncertain returns, and may make it harder to maintain quality. The liberal turn has not attracted overseas investors.

A broader understanding of the changes might move beyond a narrow party-political or short-term economic approach to a political economy which examines the linkages between economic context and political ideas. From this perspective, the restructuring can be seen as having a further and more radical objective. This is to embed the reforms and achieve a lasting change in the political climate of the UK.

Cuts plus restructuring: imposing a radical liberalism? From this perspective the current programme is also designed to embed a permanent shift to the right in British politics and at the same time move towards a solution to the long-run problem of Britain's relative economic decline.

Britain was uniquely successful as the first industrial nation in the early and mid-nineteenth century. It then experienced relative decline as competitors who developed their own industries in a world where they had to compete successfully with the first-comer emerged (for discussion, see Childs 2001). The position of the British economy fell further behind during the struggles between the imperial powers in the first quarter and between the industrial powers during the second quarter of the twentieth century. The period of US hegemony after the Second World War enabled stable growth, although the relative economic position of the country continued to fall behind that of leading capitalist powers such as Germany, Japan and the US. The ending of the cold war and rise of the new industrial leaders in Asia and South America in an intensely competitive world drives home the problem. Government must find a way forward for Britain PLC.

Various approaches have been tried during the past half-century. None has managed to combine secure economic success and sustained electoral support. They include Harold Wilson's attempt to develop a new planned high-tech industrialism, forged in the 'white heat of technology', imitating French and German achievements; the deregulated, deindustrialised market model of Margaret Thatcher; and the Blair/ Brown social investment 'third way', seeking to improve human capital by taxing the profits of a loosely regulated but flourishing financial sector. From this perspective, the Coalition's approach marks a decisive shift in economic direction, but draws on previous trends. New Labour from 1997 accepted the logic of the market and followed the Thatcher/ Major approach of promoting the financial sector as a major driver of

DOI: 10.1057/9781137328113

growth (Skidelsky 2012). As this sector expanded it became an increasingly powerful lobby for favourable treatment and benefited from low taxes and limited control.

New Labour did not accept the assumption that government has little to contribute to the success of the UK in increasingly competitive international markets. The early 2000s were characterised by substantial social investment in education and health care, discussed in more detail in Chapters 3 and 4. Education provision expanded across the range from early years through to school sixth forms, further education colleges and undergraduate and postgraduate programmes. Extra resources were directed to improve standards among those on lower incomes, with some success. Tax and pension credits and other benefits arrested the long-term trend to impoverishment at the bottom. A minimum wage was introduced and employment rights for individuals (for example, parental leave, employment protection and health and safety), but not collective unions rights (for example, a repeal of the strict regulation of industrial action introduced in the 1980s), improved to European standards.

These policies did very little to restrain the escalation of incomes at the top. They did achieve a slowdown in the relative decline among lower earners and reduced the numbers in poverty. The proportion of individuals with incomes below the 60 per cent of average income poverty line (after housing costs), which had remained above 24 per cent for the late 1980s and the whole of the 1990s, fell to 21 per cent between 1996–7 and 2003–4 (DWP 2012c, table 3.1tr). They also improved opportunities in education and in the workplace. The National Equalities Panel report shows a narrowing in the gap between children's attainment in school, whether measured by social class position or entitlement to free school meals, during the early 2000s. The gender gap, driven by cumulative social changes as well as by social policy, narrowed more rapidly (NEP 2010, 276).

The new approach was intended to produce a market-friendly welfare state that would both encourage growth and promote equality of opportunity and shift the balance away from individualism towards greater social cohesion. Current policies weaken the regulation of the market further, cutting back individual workplace rights and enforcing incentives. Government takes less responsibility for human capital and social infrastructure. Policies to mitigate poverty and promote social cohesion are curtailed. Taxes are kept as low as possible. Social

DOI: 10.1057/9781137328113

provision is designed around the imperatives of strengthening work incentives and promoting individual enterprise. The outcome is benefit cuts, stricter limits on entitlement, determined measures to reduce poverty traps for those who still receive benefits, harsh work incentives and competitive markets across all welfare services open to all qualified providers with greater opportunities for entrepreneurs: a decisive shift towards vigorous and inegalitarian liberalism. Britain moves away from a European style of welfare state towards the US model, a process dramatised in the gradient of projected public spending from 2012 in Figure 1.2 and reflecting the move towards a US pattern of inequality in Figure 2.4. In this model a generous and inclusive welfare state has no part to play.

Making the cuts permanent: The grand trajectory of government expenditure during the past two centuries in the UK and in most developed countries is upwards. Spending typically fluctuates around a particular level in the short term, but then rises, driven by systemic shocks such as major wars. The only permanent contractions since the 1850s have been in the immediate aftermath of conflicts. Public spending in the UK hovered around 10 per cent of GDP during the second half of the nineteenth century, rose to 20 per cent during the Boer war, fell back to 15 per cent, peaked at 55 per cent during the First World War, then fell back to around 30 per cent, reached 70 per cent during the Second World War and has fluctuated around 40 per cent ever since.

Various governments have attempted to cut expenditure as an act of policy, but the level of spending has proved remarkably resilient. The main periods of peace-time retrenchment in the UK are 1921–2 (the Geddes Axe), the 1931 National Coalition government cuts, the 1975 Labour cuts following the IMF loan, the Conservative cuts under Mrs Thatcher in the 1980s and under Major in the 1990s and, more recently, the spending restrictions of New Labour from 2007. The limited success of governments in achieving cutbacks and their failure to make them anything more than a temporary interruption in an overall pattern of growth has been extensively studied (Dunsire and Hood 1989, Hood *et al.* 2010, Peacock and Wiseman 1967, IFS 2011).

In all these cases the government achieved a proportion of the planned cutback (between a half and three-quarters) at the cost of conflict and civil unrest, only to find that spending returned to previous levels within five years. Pressures to restore spending come from various directions: from local government, as in the 1920s, when it was less subject to

DOI: 10.1057/9781137328113

central control than now, from concerns about civil disorder, strikes and a naval mutiny as in the 1930s, from the desire to appease voters, as in the restoration of the 1980s cuts before the 1992 election, and from the resistance of the state apparatus to contraction, as in the relatively modest 2007 Spending Review cutbacks.

Experience overseas also demonstrates the difficulties countries face in embedding permanent spending cuts. The comparative literature identifies only two cases among developed economies in the recent past: Canada in the early to mid-1990s and New Zealand a decade earlier. Both experienced major external shocks leading to foreign exchange crises as trade preference with the UK was undermined by EU regulation and as competition from newly industrialised countries reduced the Canadian share of the US market. Both countries underwent painful reform programmes which shifted their level of public spending from about 45 to 40 per cent of GDP for Canada and from 40 to 35 per cent for New Zealand. In both cases structural reforms involving the abolition of whole areas of government spending (export subsidies and insurance unemployment benefit in the case of New Zealand, a range of subsidies for farming and primary production in Canada) and massive market reforms in other areas played a key role. In most other countries cutbacks achieve a temporary fall in spending which is then restored, as it has been in previous episodes in the UK (see Taylor-Gooby 2012 for discussion).

The restructuring programme of the 2010 Coalition fragments state services and gives private market providers a much larger role. It forces state agencies in local and central government to cut and to restrict the range of their activities. The lobbies within the welfare state that defended collective provision become weaker as members of professional groups and trade unions are increasingly divided between competing employers. Local government, education, social care and NHS interest groups find their constituencies are split. At the same time powerful new lobbies for more privatisation expand and become entrenched among provider groups. It is extremely hard to dislodge these groups once in place without disrupting provision for vulnerable people, encountering adverse publicity campaigns and possibly running counter to competition law.

Re-channelling ideology: The reform package in the UK may also shift citizen's life-experience and their perceptions of their own interests towards market individualism. There are four aspects to this process.

DOI: 10.1057/9781137328113

First, the reforms undermine the collective institutions that provide leadership in articulating common concerns. The main such bodies in the UK outside government and the family are the labour movement, the voluntary sector and religion. Trade unions are in decline as a result of long-term shifts away from large-scale manufacturing employment towards a more fragmented service sector, helped by the rolling back of legislation to protect their status from the mid-1980s onwards. The outsourcing of state services to mainly non-unionised private providers weakens the movement further. The voluntary sector is under considerable pressure and is strongest in relation to a specific range of social interests, as discussed earlier. Religious groupings have become more diverse and do not typically direct their concerns towards state welfare issues. Leadership within many areas of social provision is passing to large private providers, in a strong position to lobby government. Information on the detail of contracts is covered by confidential confidentiality. It becomes harder for citizens to get good information on the quality and cost of provision.

Second, the reforms narrow interests and focus them on immediate local service providers and away from national or collective institutions. Those using the services are much more likely to think of themselves as individual consumers trying to do the best for their own families in an expanded and complex market, rather than as members of a collective body, contributing to the decisions that determine provision for the whole community. The pressures to get children into a popular school in the context of a selection mechanism run by an academy or free school rather than the local authority, the choice of a provider for one's health care from different GP-led Commissioning Groups, which have much greater autonomy in how they operate and what services they privatise, rather than by a national NHS, the transfer of complaints about social care for relatives to a private company rather than a social services department, all lead in the same direction. A further factor is the extent to which cutbacks and quality issues lead individuals to purchase some services privately.

Thirdly, the escalation of stigma discussed earlier places greater weight on the values attached to paid work, so that those on benefits are increasingly seen as a dependent underclass. These shifts go hand-in-hand with growing inequalities and deepening social divisions. The way in which welfare provision is presented and understood separates out the mass services of typical life-course needs and monitors more rigorously the more vulnerable groups on the benefits that are being cut back.

DOI: 10.1057/9781137328113

The shift in the institutional structure of the welfare state reflects and reinforces broader shifts in society. The fourth aspect is the erosion of collective support. The fanning out of inequalities described earlier provides a setting in which social sympathy between better- and worse-off groups is hard to sustain. The evidence of a more insistent stigmatisation of the poor indicates that social divisions are expressed in greater antagonism between the mass of the population and the poor as living standards diverge. At the same time life becomes more individualised and the agencies that could allow people the opportunity to recognise, articulate and act in a collective interest are increasingly undermined. Powerful new groups pursuing their immediate market interests emerge. People's social experience and their interests slide more towards the individualised self-directed logic of the market actor. In this sense, despite a lack of success in addressing underlying economic issues and finding a new and successful direction for the economy, the Coalition reforms may embed change and achieve a permanent shift to the right in the climate of ideas in the UK.

The social and economic context of the UK provides a setting in which a redirection of the political climate is possible. This is bound up with a new approach to welfare which emphasises cutbacks and restructuring designed not to save money or make services any more cost-efficient but primarily to promote the individualisation of the social world and to help assure the continued ascendancy of an ideological liberalism. In short, the reform programme is not only about exploiting social divisions to attract votes. It is underlain by the struggle between private and collective, played out in the context of the post-industrial state.

Conclusions

The UK has moved from a European to a US pattern of social inequalities as a result of shifts in labour markets, in access to education and training, in the power of capital and in other factors. These shifts combine with currents in public opinion and in mass politics that strengthen social divisions and erode support for inclusive welfare. The new context provides the opportunity for government to move decisively against the welfare state tradition and towards a new more individualistic liberalism. Whether such an approach will be any more successful than market-centred initiatives have in the recent past is unclear. It ignores

DOI: 10.1057/9781137328113

the arguments for state investment to generate growth, for investment in human capital and for inclusive social provision that are central to the case for a strong welfare state.

This chapter reviews the social and political context of the current programme of cutbacks plus restructuring. It shows that political explanations of why the government embarked on this programme have some strength but are unconvincing, as the new directions appear unable to command stable electoral support, guarantee savings or attract overseas investment. The alternative is to understand the new policies as part of a project to embed cuts permanently and shift political values in support of a new radical liberalism as a solution to Britain's long-standing economic difficulties. This explains why the set-backs for current policies have not led to dilution of the cuts and the reinstatement of state-led investment. Instead government has redoubled its efforts to cut welfare spending, especially for poorer minorities, reinforce work incentives and privatise state provision. The objective is to embed cuts and shift political ideas permanently to the right.

DOI: 10.1057/9781137328113

3
Addressing the Double Crisis: The Welfare State Trilemma

Abstract: *It is hard to promote humane, generous policies in an unequal and divided society in which most people reject tax rises and are suspicious of the poor. Proponents of a more generous welfare state face a trilemma between inclusive goals, the cost of effective policies and public antipathy to claimants. The stigmatisation of poverty rests on the beliefs that the poor are irresponsible, work-shy and contribute little. Redistributive programmes which focus on children (not seen as responsible for their own poverty) and stress the capacity of other groups of claimants to contribute to society are more feasible. These need to be combined with social investment in child and elder care and education, preventive policies and 'pre-distribution' to raise bottom-end wages and strengthen workplace rights, and can only be carried through with political commitment and determined leadership.*

Keywords: benefit reform; child poverty; contribution; living wage; pre-distribution; prevention; social investment; stigma; tax aversion; welfare state trilemma

Taylor-Gooby, Peter. *The Double Crisis of the Welfare State and What We Can Do About It.* Basingstoke: Palgrave Macmillan, 2013. DOI: 10.1057/9781137328113

Chapter 1 outlined the twin pressures on the welfare state: the immediate squeeze on spending from the economic crisis, exacerbated by the liberal market-oriented response of government; and the slow-burn crisis, as population ageing combines with wage growth in health, education and social care and with shifts in expectations to escalate the cost of providing acceptable services. Chapter 2 reviewed social and economic contexts. It showed how a number of factors (growing inequalities, wider divisions in the life-experience of different groups, declining sympathy for poor minorities, contraction of the manufacturing industrial base that had nourished labour as a political movement and concerns about the relative decline of the UK as an economic power) provide a setting favourable to a broadly pro-market redirection of the national enterprise. The liberal reforms to the welfare state fit well with a political programme designed to gain the support of middle-class groups and private sector interests. They form part of a larger project to shift the UK political economy onto a new more straightforwardly liberal course and to reinforce the individualist, anti-welfare, competitive and pro-entrepreneurial values that support such an undertaking.

A shift in political economy and in ideology requires three things: a context in which the new direction can plausibly be attractive; a political and economic logic to justify change and a social force to drive it forward: opportunity, justification and support. Thatcher seized on the disarray of the 1970s government, pursued the logic that 'public spending is at the heart of Britain's economic difficulties' (HM Treasury 1979, para 1), and mobilised aspirational upper working class groups alongside traditional core Conservative voters. Blair in 1979 drew on the sense of national decline, offered a 'Third Way' approach which combined human capital-led growth with higher social spending and attracted support from middle as well as working class groups. In the current context the banking crisis and economic stagnation provide the first, an analysis that focuses on state spending and a high deficit as the central factors undermining national competitiveness the second, and the qualms of 'comfortable Britain', reinforced by business interests in a more privatised system, the third.

The new direction is more likely to prosper in the absence of feasible alternatives and of effective resistance. This chapter and the next consider why the left and social democrats find it so difficult to develop a feasible programme for the defence and development of the welfare state. They go on to examine the kinds of policies that might be successful in

DOI: 10.1057/9781137328113

advancing a humane and generous welfare state in the face of the double crisis. In this chapter we deal mainly with the vertically redistributive minority services which face the toughest challenges since these services attract least support from the mass public. Chapter 4 addresses issues in relation to horizontal redistribution in mass provision for health and social care, education and pensions.

The pro-welfare trilemma

A successful programme to advance the welfare state must meet three conditions:

▸ Provision must be generous and inclusive, and must establish conditions that help lead the climate of public debate towards collective rather than individual perspectives on future policy, otherwise the programme will not establish a humane welfare state.

▸ It must be feasible in the sense that it commands the electoral support needed to sustain the programme; otherwise it has no future.

▸ It must be effective in delivering the outcomes desired, otherwise there is no point.

These three conditions make up a trilemma: meeting any two precludes the third. Generous and inclusive services which are effective are likely to be unpopular. British voters are generally tax averse and better services require more resources. Such services must also confront the suspicions that many people feel for the undeserving poor. They are therefore politically unfeasible. Conversely generous and inclusive services that are feasible are likely to be ineffective, since they must pare benefits down to the level that tax-payers find acceptable and impose such stringent entitlement conditions, to ensure that benefits go only to the deserving poor, that some vulnerable people are excluded. By the same token effective and feasible services find it hard to be generous.

From the viewpoint of those who wish to advance a more humane welfare state, effectiveness requires that reforms lead towards future support for more inclusive provision, rather than reinforcing divisions between those who see themselves as net contributors and those they define as dependent. Equally, a humane and generous welfare system must meet and be seen to meet the needs felt by the mass of tax-payers,

DOI: 10.1057/9781137328113

not just excluded low-income minorities. Effective provision must both meet needs and address the problem of escalating cost. This returns us to the problem of the resources required to finance inclusive provisions for lower-income minorities and to maintain standards in mass services.

Those who are not committed to high standards in collective social provision face no such problems. From the liberal standpoint there is no requirement to be generous and inclusive, since only the most extreme market outcomes are to be mitigated. Welfare must be designed to maintain provision for supporters and enhance work incentives as cheaply as possible. Cutbacks presented as good housekeeping that avoids debt, guarantees lower taxes and directs the bulk of the cuts to out-groups can be popular and therefore feasible. Effectiveness is not measured by generosity and inclusiveness, but is much more a matter of limited interventionism, promotion of work incentives and meeting the needs of groups likely to support the programme.

In the context of the immediate crisis, the test for those committed to state welfare is to devise a programme that will meet both short-term and longer-term needs across all groups of citizens without very large increases in tax, and that can command electoral support. For the long-run crisis any solution must contain spending but sustain highly popular services and make them more inclusive. These are severe challenges. We now consider the three aspects of the trilemma (generosity and inclusiveness, electoral feasibility and effectiveness in delivering the goods) as they affect welfare for low-income minorities in more detail.

Generosity and inclusiveness

In this section we examine two obstacles to generous and inclusive policies: first, the division between strong public support for the services such as health care, education and pensions and the much more stigmatic attitudes towards unemployed people, single parents and the poor; second, entrenched resistance to higher taxes, aided by misconceptions about the cost of high-quality provision and the level and progressiveness of taxation.

Stigma and the welfare state: Figure 3.1 illustrates the problem. Drawn from the authoritative British Social Attitudes survey dataset it shows that support for more government spending on social provision has fallen during the past two decades and particularly since the early

DOI: 10.1057/9781137328113

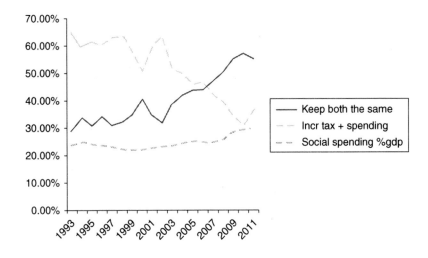

FIGURE 3.1   *Attitudes to tax and spending and proportion of GDP spent on pensions, health, education and welfare for the poor, 1993–2011 (BSA)*

Note: Social spending is defined as 'health, education, and welfare'.

Source: www.britsocat.com at the Centre for Comparative European Survey Data.

2000s, from a comfortable majority of about 60 per cent of the population to about 30 per cent, with a slight upturn between 2009 and 2010 as the recession bit home. Public attitudes are the mirror image of actual spending which has risen steadily, as we showed in Chapter 1. A clear majority now want spending and tax to stay as they are, while the proportion in favour of real spending cuts so that tax can be cut back has risen. This pattern is corroborated by data from other surveys and by the increased caution with which politicians have approached spending rises during the period.

The point that it is spending directed at poverty and inequality that is viewed with the deepest suspicion is emphasised in answers to further questions about people's top priority for more spending, assuming the money was available. Figure 3.2 shows how education and health care are far and away the leading priorities, with 30 per cent of those interviewed consistently supporting more education spending and the proportion for health above 40 per cent, and exceeding 50 per cent in the early 2000s. Support for more spending on the NHS declined somewhat after the big increases of the early 2000s, when the 2003 rise in N.I. contributions provided an extra £8bn for the service. Social housing and cash benefits

DOI: 10.1057/9781137328113

receive very low levels of support, with some upturn for housing as rents started to escalate from about 2005 onwards.

The survey deals with priorities for the various social benefits in a separate question. This is a complex field and one where responses tend to be overshadowed by the far greater enthusiasm for the NHS if it is included in the same question. Figure 3.3 gives available data for the period 1993 to 2010.

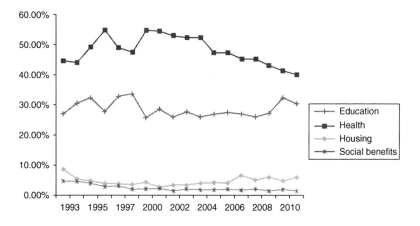

FIGURE 3.2   *Top priorities for social spending, 1993–2011 (BSA)*
Source: as Figure 3.1.

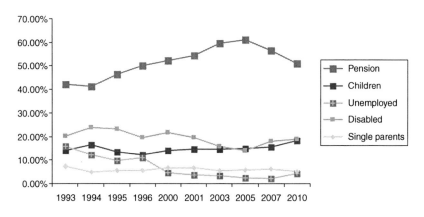

FIGURE 3.3   *Top priorities for spending on cash benefits, 1993–2011 (BSA)*
Source: as Figure 3.2.

DOI: 10.1057/9781137328113

The main contrast lies between pensions, far and away the most popular (and highest spending) cash benefit, and benefits for unemployed people. Pensions enjoyed increasing priority up to 2005, with some decline afterwards as the extra money for the Guaranteed Minimum Pension improved benefits somewhat. The downward trajectory of support for unemployment benefits parallels that on spending to relieve poverty discussed in relation to stigma in Chapter 2. Single parents receive very little support and benefits for children are rated a priority by about 15 per cent of those interviewed, but support here rises during the 2000s. Support for sick and disabled people has fallen but recovered somewhat after 2005.

These data show that the number of people who favour increases in welfare state spending has fallen sharply. Health care, education and pensions are by far the most popular services, but it is not clear that many people are willing to pay extra taxes for higher spending even in these areas. There is a clear division between these mass services and services directed at poverty, such as social housing and unemployment benefits. The latter are priorities for very few people indeed, and support has fallen in recent years. The only group for whom backing has risen, from a low base, seems to be children, during a period in which Child Tax Credits (and also services in kind through Sure Start day-care, early entrance to education and better workplace rights for parents) have been promoted by government. The picture overall is one of division rather than inclusion and one which fits in with the growing stigmatisation of poverty among people of working age discussed in Chapter 2.

There is considerable academic discussion of why some benefits are unpopular and why some claimers attract stigma. One explanation is simple self-interest: more people hope to live to old age and enjoy pensions, while unemployment is concentrated among lower-skilled workers and for most is fairly brief. Other explanations rest on social values. Four common factors predominate in studies of the low esteem in which benefits that redistribute to the poor of working age and the people who get them are held (van Oorschot 2000, Cook 1979, Coughlin 1980, Mau 2004):

▸ Need for benefits, usually seen as breadline poverty rather than just falling below an arbitrarily defined poverty line;
▸ Responsibility for the contingency that leads to the need, so that it is in some sense one's 'fault' (for example, unwillingness to take any job offered), and allied to this, the extent to which the claimer acknowledges responsibility and take steps to address it;

DOI: 10.1057/9781137328113

- ▶ Reciprocity in the sense of previous or potential contribution to society (for example, social insurance contributions or work record); and
- ▶ Membership of a group with whom the citizen identifies.

Needs are real for many groups. The least deserving are typically those whose poverty is not immediately obvious, who don't seem to take responsibility for their dependence, who fail to make any contribution to society in return for welfare and who are socially most distant from the mass of the population, whether through ethnicity, values, life-style or contact.

These values form the basis for a common hierarchy of need groups in most developed countries. People tend to be most concerned about the elderly, the sick and disabled, then the unemployed, and finally immigrants. Services like health care and education are highly valued because they meet mass needs for which people do not feel themselves responsible, which, especially in the case of education, help people to contribute to society, and which are typically seen as relevant to everyone. Public support for social spending in different areas follows the order of priority in Figures 3.2 and 3.3. The pattern is explained by the perceived deservingness of the different groups, particularly how far they are responsible for their need or contribute to society, and whether they are groups with whom most people can identify. Analyses of large cross-national surveys such as the International Social Survey Project, European Social Survey and World Values Survey confirm the pattern (Jaeger 2007, 89, Svallfors 2004, Taylor-Gooby 2002, van Oorschot 2006). Paid work combines taking responsibility, making a contribution and living as most people do. The main current in social values supports the work ethic. Social divisions aided by the rhetoric surrounding work-centred welfare reinforce this.

A number of factors have contributed to the growth of stigma during recent years. Support for public spending overall has declined. Within that pattern the divisions between the different services and especially between pensions and benefits for unemployed people remain substantial, with a recent indication of somewhat greater support for children, sick and disabled people and those in need of housing in the recession. Until 2010 public spending had risen. The benefits system has increasingly stressed work tests with ever more stringent pressure on unemployed people to retrain and to pursue vigorously every opening. The onus is placed squarely on claimers, and they are by implication responsible

DOI: 10.1057/9781137328113

for their needs because they have failed to take full advantage of the opportunities. The leading characteristic of the new Universal Credit system listed on the DWP website is that it will 'improve work incentives'. Addressing poverty comes fourth on the list after the impact on the labour market and greater transparency. The accompanying White Paper links poverty and welfare dependency in the first sentence and gives the objective of reform as 'reintroducing the culture of work in households where it may have been absent for generations' (DWP 2010, 6). In fact, as noted in Chapter 1, the majority of working-age people below the poverty line live in households where at least one member is in paid work. Nonetheless, public discourse typically draws a sharp distinction between claimants and what are often termed 'hard-working families'. Greater inequality and the accompanying social divisions mean that the mass of the population is less likely to identify with the poor.

Antipathy to higher taxes: When asked about the principles that should underlie policy, most people broadly favour progressive taxation and believe that government should promote greater equality. Figure 3.4 gives the data from one of a number of British Social Attitudes survey questions on the topic. It shows that those who see the role of government as redistribution from better- to worse-off clearly predominated in the mid-1990s. Groups in favour of and against these policies have

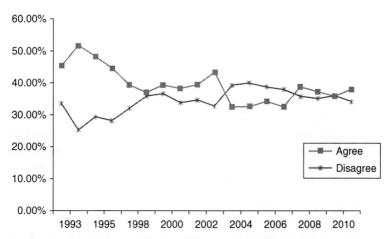

FIGURE 3.4   *Should government redistribute income from better-off to worse-off? 1993–2011 (BSA)*

Note: Agree = 'strongly agree' plus 'agree'; disagree = 'strongly disagree' plus 'disagree'.

Source: as Figure 3.1.

DOI: 10.1057/9781137328113

grown more equal during the early 2000s with a slight shift back towards redistribution as recession impacted on incomes in 2011. As in other areas, the established trend to a decline in support for redistribution is somewhat moderated by current experience.

Attitudes to the taxation necessary to finance public spending are complex, with responses varying according to the kind of tax under discussion and the context in which the question is asked (Orton and Rowlingson 2007, 25, Prabhakar 2012). Support for redistributive taxation as a matter of principle does not necessarily feed through into assumptions about policy. Many people fail to make a strong link between more spending and higher taxes, so that they will endorse both improvements to valued services, such as health care and education, and tax cuts (Hedges and Bromley 2001). When pressed, they often argue that government is inherently wasteful and that greater efficiency will solve the problem (Taylor-Gooby and Hastie 2002). The efforts devoted to cost-efficiency in public services discussed in Chapter 1 indicate that the state sector is likely to be at least as efficient as any viable alternative. Coupled with a widespread belief that Britain is a highly taxed country and that taxation is currently progressive, tax attitudes militate against major reforms to raise more revenue or reduce inequality.

Both perceptions are misleading (Horton and Gregory 2009, 100–2). The data presented in Chapter 1 show how tax-financed public spending in Britain never rose above the mid-point for the major developed countries and is now sinking to the bottom. Direct taxes reduce the main measure of inequality, the Gini coefficient, by a relatively small amount, from .376 to .342. Indirect taxes effectively cancel this out, raising the coefficient back to .377. Benefits directed at the poor have a much greater effect, cutting the coefficient from .546 to .376 (Adam and Browne 2010, 7). We noted in Chapter 2 that Britain has low social security contributions compared to most European countries. This limits the income earmarked for social benefits and means that an important connection between contributions and entitlement to benefits is lacking.

When people are asked about redistribution in practical rather than abstract terms, they find it difficult to identify from whom the extra resources should come. Hedges and Bromley's work for the Fabian Society Commission on Taxation and Citizenship (2001) showed that most people identify a group comfortably above their own income level as those who should pay more, setting the threshold at some £100,000

DOI: 10.1057/9781137328113

a year in 2000. More recent work indicates that the pattern persists and that the threshold rises with incomes (Bamfield and Horton 2009, 36).

Most people think they pay too much tax and would rather see higher taxes for other income groups (British Social Attitudes survey: Taylor-Gooby 2009, chapter 9). Attitudes to this issue have also shifted over time. The proportion thinking those on high incomes pay too much tax rose from 18 to 27 per cent and the proportion thinking they pay too little fell from 45 to 36 per cent between 1991 and 2009. Conversely, the proportion thinking that low-income people paid too much tax fell from 82 to 75 per cent; less than 2 per cent thought they paid too little. Most people think that the poor are not overtaxed, but substantial groups believe that the mass of the population higher up the income scale pay too much. This reflects the diminishing enthusiasm for redistribution shown in Figure 3.4.

Taken together these findings indicate real problems in increasing taxation at a time of severe pressures on government spending. They show why benefits for the poor and redistribution are the weakest elements in the politics of the welfare state. As the cost of the more popular services meeting lifetime needs rises, welfare for those at the bottom is squeezed, creating further distance between this group and the mass and exacerbating stigma and social division. The dominant policy response to the short-term crisis accelerates the process: the Coalition imposes cuts chiefly on benefits and services for those at the bottom and seeks to protect mass provision. Public attitudes endorse this pattern. Any viable approach to defend, let alone expand humane, generous and inclusive policies must confront these obstacles, and move away from traditional tax and spend approaches to redistribution.

There are two counter-indications to the above pattern. First public opinion is beginning to identify a group of 'undeserving rich' who contravene the values that justify allocation. They behave in an irresponsible way, their life-styles differ so markedly from those of the mass that identification with them is impossible, their actions, particularly in financial markets and in tax avoidance, appear to damage rather than contribute to British society and they don't in any sense need the money (Rowlingson and Connor 2011). Whether mass opinion will move to support the demands for higher taxes on this group advanced by the Occupy movement (Milkman *et al.* 2012) and others (Glasgow Media Group 2010) and endorsed in political calls for windfall taxation on banking profits and a 'mansion tax' is uncertain. It is also unclear how effectively taxes can be imposed on wealthy and influential people and how much money would be raised.

DOI: 10.1057/9781137328113

The second point concerns the shift in the attitude data toward greater sympathy for spending on social housing, unemployed, sick and disabled people and children and for redistribution since 2010. While this shift is too recent to constitute an established trend it may presage a reversal of the longer-term decline of the past two decades in support for state spending, particularly that directed to the most needy groups. This is reinforced by evidence of growing insecurity: Ipsos-Mori polling shows that three-fifths of the population expect the spending cuts to affect their families in the immediate future (Ipsos-Mori 2012).

Despite minor more positive indications, this section shows that many people regard the poor with suspicion, and that the current of public opinion is set firmly against higher taxes to pay for more generous and inclusive welfare. In this context reformers have suggested a number of approaches that might lead in a more generous and inclusive direction. We consider how new programmes that redistribute to those on low incomes might be designed to attract more public support.

Feasibility and effectiveness

The second aspect of the trilemma concerns feasibility: pursuing positive reform in a way that does not damage electoral support. The third concerns effectiveness: delivering the goods that those who wish to advance a humane welfare state would recognise as desirable. Feasibility and effectiveness are bound up together. Current policies to tackle the immediate crisis impose severe cuts on services and benefits for lower-income groups and widen social divisions. They build on the negative social values surrounding welfare for the poor. The problem is to make policies that work in delivering inclusiveness and generosity acceptable to the mass of the population.

The fact that any move in a more inclusive direction will involve more spending and higher taxes complicates the problem. Children cannot be seen as responsible for their own poverty. Investment in childhood may bring a reciprocal return in later life. This group is least likely to be stigmatised. They are a much higher priority for benefit spending than unemployed people or single parents (Figure 3.3). Higher spending to tackle child poverty may be acceptable to many voters.

A rough assessment based on recent work by DWP indicates that in 2008–9 some 22 per cent of the 12.8 million children in the UK lived in households whose income fell below the 60 per cent of median income poverty line before housing costs (Gardiner and Evans 2011). The mean poverty gap (the distance by which living standards fell below the line, then valued at about £12,700 a year: DWP 2012, figure 4.1) for children in 2008–9 was 30 per cent. In other words some £3800 a year would be required on average to eliminate poverty for each child. This puts the cost of eradicating child poverty in that year through redistributive benefits alone in excess of £10bn, very roughly consonant with Hirsch's estimate of £4.2bn to meet the target of halving child poverty by 2010 (Hirsch 2009). Any practicable strategy would include better wages, working conditions, employment opportunities (especially for women) and childcare, to raise living standards in low-paid families and cut the direct cost of redistributive benefits targeted on children. Benefits are more effective in addressing child poverty if claimed by the person responsible for the childcare (typically the mother) rather than the chief earner (as in Universal Credit). In cases where benefits are paid to mothers, children's living standards tend to be higher (Goode et al. 1998, Ward-Batts 2008).

More would be required to address poverty among adults. Some 5.5 million working-age adults and 2 million pensioners fell below the line in 2010–11, rising by 1.7 million if housing costs are included, according to the most recent official statistics (DWP 2012c, Tables 5.3tr and 6.3tr). Assuming that similar sums to those for child poverty were required to meet their needs, the cost of eliminating adult poverty for those of working age is in the region of £28bn, about a quarter of the existing budget for all benefits apart from pensions. The current programme of increases in the basic pension will reduce poverty among older people.

The social security cuts of 2010 and 2012 sum to nearly £22bn. The £10bn required to address child poverty is roughly half the cost of Child Tax Credits in 2009–10 (Browne and Hood 2012, table 2.1) or about 0.7 per cent of GDP. Financing benefits that would eliminate poverty among children presents tough challenges. Tackling social inclusion among adults of working age through redistribution would require three times the resources and is not politically feasible. The weakness in revenue-raising of the British welfare system derived from strong tax aversion and the limitations of an approach that raises relatively little through social insurance discussed earlier contributes to the problem. A practicable longer-term programme might address child poverty largely through direct redistribution, but combine this with other approaches to reduce

DOI: 10.1057/9781137328113

poverty among adults. Policies which might gain a purchase on popular attitudes are considered below.

There are two broad directions among current proposals. The first works with current values and seeks to redefine those receiving benefit in terms of responsibility and reciprocity and present them as people with whose lives and aspirations the mass can better identify. It also reinforces the linkage between a broader conception of contribution and entitlement. The second moves beyond the individual morality surrounding benefits and poverty and emphasises new policy directions (social investment, prevention and pre-distribution) that address the issues without making major demands on public spending.

I. Reframing redistributive welfare

Taking responsibility and making a contribution: One prominent stream in recent work stresses the idea that welfare claimers also contribute to society and that their lives and aspirations are similar to those of the rest of the population. The objective is to build on the value of reciprocity to erode stigma. Work in social anthropology, political science, decision theory and social policy demonstrates the importance of reciprocal contribution across a broad range of social relationships. Mauss' analysis of the role of gifting ceremonies in linking together groups in Inuit and in pre-colonial African societies explores reciprocity as way of managing conflicts over resources (1922). Even in the hard-nosed relationships studied in the individualised experiments of decision theory, people respond to the behaviour of others in a reciprocal way (Gintis *et al.* 2005). Market reciprocity is one of the basic components of Western societies (Durkheim 1984). Titmuss' work on blood donorship (1970) and Mau's on social insurance (2004) show how powerful institutionalised reciprocity is in providing a firm basis for welfare entitlements and welfare citizenship.

Reciprocity also emerges as a theme in survey findings on attitudes to welfare: those who are seen to make a contribution in return for their entitlement are generally favoured as deserving. Policies which draw on this theme seek to address the lack of sympathy on the part of the middle mass for those at the bottom by presenting benefit recipients as members of groups who have made or currently make contributions to society, including that through low-paid work, or who are likely to contribute in the future. This makes it harder to see them as simply a dependent out-group. Three recent proposals build on these ideas.

DOI: 10.1057/9781137328113

Horton and Gregory seek to reconcile commitment to universalism with the realities of the distinction between deserving and undeserving poor by redesigning the benefit system to incorporate as many groups as practicably possible. They propose an expansion of tax credits into what would be effectively a citizen's income for those on low incomes, structured to place the emphasis on social contribution. This would be reinforced by a combined housing benefit that covers subsidies to both lower-income tenants and home owners (2009, 216). They describe the perceived connection between contribution and entitlement in the national insurance system as 'psychological gold dust'. At the centre of their programme is an expansion of the core idea into a much more inclusive theme of social participation. Benefit entitlement for those in paid work would be based on work participation and paid contributions. This reverses current plans which remove any link between national insurance contribution and entitlement to benefits for those of working age and expand the role of means-testing as a direct test of dependence.

In the proposed system entitlement for those of working age would rest on social participation, including unwaged social care for children or frail older or disabled family members, voluntary work and training that enables a future contribution to society. Drawing on research by Sefton (2005) and others and their own work they argue that reciprocity has become increasingly central to popular ideas about desert for welfare. Most people recognise full-time caring for children, frail elderly or sick and disabled relatives, full-time studying for useful qualifications and some kinds of full-time voluntary activity as important contributions (Horton and Gregory 2009, 201–3). These activities would form the basis of an inclusive welfare state. There would be real sanctions for claimers who refuse opportunities to engage in these activities, demonstrating that the proposals are about building reciprocity rather than subsidising voluntary dependency. In relation to social values, the objective is to demonstrate that benefit claimers are often also part of the social enterprise, and that their willingness to engage in retraining, voluntary work-related activities and other areas demonstrates a commitment to take responsibility for their own needs. Contribution also enlarges the capacity of the state to raise the funds to pay for welfare and strengthens the sense of entitlement among both contributors and recipients.

This is an ambitious proposal to construct a universal inclusive welfare state by reinforcing relationships of reciprocity rather than moralistic divisions or individual interests. Real problems lie in ensuring that the

DOI: 10.1057/9781137328113

mass public understand the entitlement of those out of work as justified by current activities intended to help contribute to society.

A less far-reaching proposal from Bell and Gaffney (2012) also builds on the current National Insurance system to strengthen the contributory principle. This proposal does not confront public attitudes which stigmatise the dependent poor directly but seeks to define a much larger group of claimants than at present as contributors. The coverage of an enhanced National Insurance scheme could be broadened by crediting parental leave and childcare, caring for sick or disabled relatives and training. The current Lower Earnings Limit which excludes low-paid workers from making contributions would be abolished. The system of National Insurance benefits, phased out from 2013, would be reinstated and expanded through higher entitlements to ensure that claimers did not also need means-tested top-ups. The link between contribution and entitlement would become more visible.

The authors point out that such a scheme could only be one part of a feasible and effective social security programme, and that it would depend on changes to the labour market to promote better-paid employment opportunities for those at the bottom so that they could pay more in contributions. They argue that the contributory principle offers a way of addressing the decline in public confidence in the welfare state and point out that the European countries that rely on social insurance were rather more successful in encouraging labour market participation in the early 2000s.

A further and more limited contributory approach is the national salary insurance scheme advanced by James Purnell (see Cooke 2011). Workers whose employment is interrupted by illness or redundancy would receive a relatively high benefit which could be recouped through a tax supplement on their return to work. This is essentially a loan system underwritten by the state rather than a benefit or insurance. The problem is that it is hard to devise a scheme that would not reinforce social divisions. Skilled workers with relatively low risk of unemployment and short periods between jobs might benefit. However lower-skilled more marginal workers who are the first to lose work in a recession would be unable to pay off the loan and would not be included. The scheme entrenches the deserving/undeserving distinction among claimants (Baumberg 2012).

Contribution schemes face a dilemma. The more inclusive they become, the less clearly they are contribution based and the more they cost. The more they are limited to groups who might be able to finance decent benefits for themselves from lifetime contributions, the harder it is to include low-skilled people and the other groups most vulnerable in the labour market. Contributory schemes then consolidate stigmatic social divisions. Horton and Gregory do not cost their scheme. It is hard to produce a realistic estimate since the amounts involved depend on how people might behave during job search and in pursuit of higher wages under a more universal system, as well as the current depth of poverty among different population groups. In addition current policy changes move the goalposts by cutting back entitlements and targeting benefits more narrowly, which raises the cost of any genuinely inclusive reform. A contributory approach could form part of an inclusive response to working-age poverty, but could only be developed gradually. It would need reinforcement from other policies, such as more direct redistribution, targeted at child poverty.

Responsibility and children: An alternative to approaches which seek to reframe the need for welfare by stressing the contribution that those on benefits make to society focuses on issues of responsibility and identity. The proposals considered above include responsibility by establishing a 'welfare to work' programme for unemployed claimers. They address the issue of the social distance between claimers and non-claimers by expanding the group of claimers and positing normal life-course roles (childcare, elder care, volunteering as well as paid work) as grounds for entitlement. The perspective now considered questions how far claimers can be held responsible for their poverty, by focusing attention on families and children and on those in paid work.

An influential 1960s poverty lobby group chose to call itself the 'Child Poverty Action Group' to emphasise the way poverty affects children and to stress its activist rather than academic role. Although children make up a minority among the poor, the incidence of poverty among children is higher (at 19.6 per cent) than among parents (17 per cent) or childless adults of working age (15.1 per cent: Brewer *et al.* 2011, 2). Child poverty attracts greater public sympathy. The 2010 Child Poverty Act sets targets for the reduction and finally eradication of child poverty by 2020. The popularity of this measure is indicated by the fact that it remains a government target despite cutbacks in child benefit, tax credit and housing benefit and new policies which are likely to increase child poverty (DWP 2012b), although the at the time of writing DWP is seeking to redefine poverty (DWP 2012h).

DOI: 10.1057/9781137328113

Children cannot be blamed for their poverty. Family life is an aspiration with which most people identify. The tax credit policies of the 1997–2010 Labour government addressed poverty through a means-tested supplement to income. The initial credits were paid in 2003 for children, low-income working families and pensioners but were later extended to cover disabled people, childcare costs and other needs. A key feature of tax credit was the move towards greater social inclusion. The credits were paid through the tax system which applied to the mass of the working population rather than by a separate benefits agency. They were available both to those out of work and those in work. They stressed the needs of children. Perhaps most importantly the income threshold rose progressively to £42,000 by 2009–10. This was considerably above median national income of £27,250 a year for a couple in full-time work and £17,850 for a couple with one member working (2010–11 statistics, DWP 2012c, table 2.3ts).

The object was to include the mass of the population in the benefit system and promote stronger identity between working and non-working groups. Support for children was the main element in the policies to expand welfare. As the attitude data presented earlier showed, the expansion of tax credits, spearheaded by Child Tax Credit, took place at a time when support for social spending was in decline and most people were increasingly suspicious of claimers, but support for children as top priority for extra public spending rose by a third between 2003 and 2011, faster than in any other area. Child poverty fell from 2.9 to 2.3 million between 2003 and 2010. Nonetheless the 2010 poverty target of 1.7 million was substantially exceeded. Child benefit has been frozen and removed from the better-off and Child Tax Credit cut back by the current government. The tax credits will be included within Universal Credit and subjected to work tests.

The relative success of policies that took the focus away from work issues and foregrounded child poverty indicates that family-centred approaches have the potential to address poverty in ways that circumvent the negative values attached to welfare. Child and Working Tax Credits cost some £27bn by 2009–10. Extending these schemes to eradicate poverty in a more universal approach to welfare citizenship would entail very real costs, more than a third as much again for child poverty, according to the estimate presented earlier. However, the success of previous programmes in this field indicates that child poverty is the most hopeful area for humane and inclusive redistributive welfare.

DOI: 10.1057/9781137328113

So far the discussion has been framed in terms of individual morality and behaviour, to do with responsibility, identity and contribution to society. Other reform proposals consider broader social analyses of poverty and its causes. They address the need for welfare as the outcome of societal processes rather than individual behaviour and fall into three main groups, to do with social investment, prevention and pre-distribution.

II. Moving beyond redistribution

Social investment: Here the argument is that structural factors prevent the optimum use of resources by the economy. Labour is one of the four basic factors of production listed in most economics texts alongside land, physical capital and enterprise. Policies to improve the quality of labour as human capital or enhance its utilisation attract much support but insufficient resources. In the UK, the Leitch report called for more spending on education, especially on lifelong learning to boost productivity and create 'a more prosperous and fairer society' (Leitch 2006, 4). At the European level the first Lisbon Treaty in 2000 set out the vision of making Europe 'the most competitive and dynamic knowledge-based economy in the world, capable of sustainable economic growth with more and better jobs and greater social cohesion' (EU 2000, 5). This objective links economic and social progress in the same breath and gives a prominent role to human capital. These ideals are developed in work on social investment (Morel *et al.* 2011), which points out that social divisions are deepening across Europe and calls for a state investment strategy centred on education and training but including spending on childcare and social support to enable full and equal participation in work.

The value of investment is reinforced by authoritative research which demonstrates the advantage of middle over working class over lower working class children in educational performance before schooling at age three and shows how the class and income differences widen up to age 14 as schooling progresses (NEP 2010, figure 11.15). The ambitious Canadian *Better Beginnings, Better Futures* programme (Peters *et al.* 2010) demonstrates that early childhood education can produce lasting results. An approach which succeeded in improving skill levels across the population would not only mitigate inequalities, but also enhance national productive capacity, including that of disadvantaged groups. Here UK

DOI: 10.1057/9781137328113

policy has moved in two main directions: fragmentation of the system to provide more space for local autonomy in the Academy (Adonis 2012) and more recently Free School programmes; and targeted initiatives to improve standards among lower-income groups in the early 2000s (the London Challenge, Excellence in Cities and Education Action Zones).

The evidence on the first direction in reform is at best equivocal: academies and free schools may enhance standards for some groups but do little to mitigate inequalities (Fiske and Ladd 2000, Gibbons *et al.* 2006). The increased freedom of such schools over curriculum, teaching methods and, implicitly, recruitment are likely to widen inequalities in the future. There was some success in particular initiatives involving targeted spending in raising standards in schools in deprived areas and among lower-income students in the early 2000s. For example, the rate of improvement at GCSE was higher in Excellence in Cities schools. Students were more than twice as likely to obtain five good GCSEs, a cost-effective outcome over a four-year period for an average of about £500 per pupil (DCSF 2007, 5). The deprivation premium was increased faster than the basic allowance: in schools where a third or more of children receive free meals, the proportion attaining at least five good GCSEs rose from about 20 to about 40 per cent between 1999 and 2005 (Lupton *et al.*, 2009, figure 4.3). Further evidence is discussed in the next chapter.

A further point concerns the linkage between better individual opportunities and improved human capital, made for example in Blair's *Third Way* strategy (Giddens 1998). Detailed analysis indicates that there is a higher return from improvements in the performance of those already close to the next threshold: investment in 'individuals in the middle of the distribution rather than at the bottom may be more (cost) effective' (Crawford *et al.* 2011, 5). This gives rise to a tension within opportunity policies for advocates of humane state welfare, between the goals of social justice and enhanced economic efficiency. Social justice is desirable in its own right, but requires extra resources beyond those justified by a strictly economic rationality.

A more direct approach seeks to identify clear economic returns to government and the economy which will immediately justify more inclusive policies. The most obvious returns are in relation to the provision of care on the grounds that this releases those engaged in informal care for children or frail relatives (over 90 per cent of them women) for more productive work that will generate taxes. The most fruitful area

DOI: 10.1057/9781137328113

is childcare, now so expensive in the UK that it imposes a real burden on single parent families and two-earner couples. The cost of part-time childcare (25 hours a week) for a two-year old exceeds £5000, with costs higher in the South-East and in London, against a minimum wage of about £12,000 a year (Daycare Trust 2012). UK childcare costs in relation to incomes are the highest among OECD countries, have risen sharply, and will rise further as Child Tax Credit and child benefits are cut back and frozen (Ben-Galim 2011, figure 1). A state scheme that provided free universal childcare could generate some £5000 a year for government in extra tax payments and benefits saved if the parents who would now be able to work earn average wages. The amount saved falls to £1250 if (as might be more likely in many cases) the new workers earn the minimum wage (Ben-Galim 2011, 15–16).

A similar argument can be made for social care for older people, although here the economic arguments may be weaker, since the generally older carers released for paid work have a looser attachment to the labour market. One study estimates that the savings from a social care service which released informal carers of frail elderly people into paid work might be £4200 each (Pickard *et al.* 2012).The moral argument in terms of mitigating the immediate burden and damage to future career prospects falling mainly on women carers is at least equally strong (Pickard, *et al.* 2012, Knapp *et al.* 2010). For these reasons investment in high-quality childcare services is a central element in the Women's Budget Group's economic recovery programme, *Plan F* (WBG 2012a).

Social investment is also discussed in a broader sense, in relation to gains from such areas as reduction of smoking or alcohol consumption or other behavioural changes to lessen pressures on the NHS, health benefits from improved social housing or public health (Compass 2011, 32). The most impressive returns on social investment are found in education (Dickson and Smith 2011) and in childcare. Outcomes are harder to quantify in other areas.

Prevention: The logic of prevention, put simply taking action in order to reduce the risk of some larger harm, follows closely that of investment, taking action to generate some anticipated larger good. It has been developed most forcibly in relation to climate change mitigation, where Stern estimates that the cost of unabated carbon emissions through their impact on global warming at some 5 per cent of GDP annually by 2050. Spending at a level as low as 1 per cent by 2020 could contain the

DOI: 10.1057/9781137328113

problem (Stern 2006). However consideration of climate change, important though it is, is beyond the scope of this book.

Prevention assumes some confidence in knowledge of future developments and in the relationship between policies and outcomes (Gough 2012). It must also allow for some discounting of a future that has not and perhaps may not arise against present uses of the resources where we can be more confident of a return. This limits the adoption of preventive strategies at a time of severe spending pressure to those where returns can be demonstrated. Understanding of the role of environment in crime prevention (Crowe 2000), the social causes of ill-health (discussed in the next chapter, see Marmot 2010, Scott and Freeman 1995), social care, education and training (as detailed above and in the next chapter) and of the 'scarring' effects of prolonged unemployment (Arulampalam *et al.* 2001) is reasonably well developed, making preventive initiatives in these cases practicable. There is good reason to believe that realistic investments in the present, in the design of housing estates, in improving the opportunities for healthy life-styles, in early detection of disease among low-income people, in improving training opportunities, and in ensuring that unemployed people retain skills and aptitudes, will generate returns over time.

Recently government policies in areas such as employment (DWP 2011b) and drug use (Home Office 2010) have experimented in combining investment with prevention. Non-state providers are contracted to produce desirable outcomes (a successful transition to employment, declining drug use in an area for a given period) for clients, and paid by results, with higher payments for higher-risk groups. The assumption is that this approach will give the providers an incentive to invest in hard to reach groups and to innovate in developing effective services, since that is how they will gain a return.

This is an imaginative response to problems of public spending since it engages and directs private capital. Results are not yet available although recent reports indicate problems in establishing a competitive market, since relatively few private suppliers come forward unless the returns appear secure and substantial, and in enforcing the contracts when recession makes the challenges tougher (DWP 2012e). There are also serious difficulties in monitoring to ensure contractors do not cherry-pick the easiest cases where they are highly confident of a return and in protecting charities which sub-contract to private providers from exploitation (NSPCC 2011, NCVO 2012). This illustrates the enormous difficulties in

DOI: 10.1057/9781137328113

making reliable predictions in these areas, where risks have previously deterred private providers, and the extra pressure such policies put on the regulatory capacity of the state.

Pre-distribution: Like prevention, the pre-distributive approach avoids conflicts over tax and spending by using the regulatory powers of government. Half a century ago, the argument runs, the mass of the population depended on manufacturing sector employment, trade unions had considerable influence, wages were rather less widely dispersed and there was much greater job security. Over time manufacturing industry has declined in importance to be replaced by service sector employment in which work situations are more diverse and the balance of power shifts to employers. The working class is more divided and has less influence in the workplace. These factors increase inequality, as discussed in Chapter 2.

New policies cannot reverse major structural shifts in the economy, but they can go some way to mitigating them. Pre-distribution addresses inequalities at source rather than taxing and redistributing to lessen them after they have arisen. The state intervenes to make market incomes more equal and shift power towards the lower-paid. The most compelling arguments for this approach rest on the claim that state welfare was most successful in the UK when the institutions to reinforce pre-distribution were at their strongest, in the 1950s and 1960s (Coats *et al.* 2012, chapters 2 and 3). Hacker (2011) points out that the massive increase in inequality in some of the most developed countries is associated with erosion of the protective institutional framework.

Pre-distribution includes a range of possible institutional changes: strengthening the bargaining position and influence of workers through stronger trade union rights and representation on works councils, legislative interventions such as enforcement of higher minimum wages or a living wage, better working conditions, employment protection or shorter working hours, measures to curb wages at the top end through reforms to remuneration systems and possibly maximum wage legislation, and interventions to control the prices of items of common consumption such as utilities, transport or food.

These measures are attractive for three reasons: they address the issue of redistributing power towards groups that have grown relatively weaker in the market; they increase the influence of institutions that might reinforce solidarity and promote greater reciprocity across groups that may then perceive a stronger common interest; and their implementation costs are perceived to be low. This does not imply they are insignificant.

DOI: 10.1057/9781137328113

As in the case of preventive policies and for outsourcing, the costs of instituting effective supervision of workplace conditions and ensuring that regulators are not 'captured' so that they increasingly see the world from the employers' perspective are not trivial. However the potential of policies such as raising the minimum wage towards a living wage to reduce poverty and inequality is substantial.

Increases in remuneration at the bottom end also have the effect of reducing entitlements to means-tested benefits and increasing income and indirect tax payments. Despite repeated claims that raising the minimum above the market level would damage employment in low-wage sectors, there is no evidence that the minimum wage had such an effect (Metcalf 2006). Minimum wage levels are negotiated between employers and union representatives, experts and civil servants on the Low Pay Commission. The living wage is calculated by academics at Loughborough University and by the Greater London Authority as the amount necessary to assure an acceptable standard of living and is somewhat higher.

The costs of moving the wage floor above the current minimum wage (£6.19 an hour from October 2012) to a living wage (£7.45) are relatively small in construction, software, computing, banking, and food production, estimated at less than 1 per cent of the total wage bill (Pennycook 2012, 2). The average wage bill in retail, bars and restaurants would rise by between 4.7 and 6.2 per cent, which would damage the viability of some businesses. The IPPR/Resolution Foundation study recommends a shift to 90 per cent of living wage levels in these areas, at a cost of between 2.0 and 2.6 per cent of the wage bill, with further increases when possible (Pennycook 2012, 3). More recent work estimates that the pay rise shared among low-income workers from a move to full living wage pay would amount to some £6.5bn, of which £3.6bn would be recouped by the Treasury in lower benefit payments and extra tax. Some £1.3bn would be added to the pay bill for public sector workers, leaving a net gain of £1.6bn, sufficient to make inroads into child poverty (IPPR 2012). However the strain this would impose on some low-wage industries suggests that the full transition is not immediately feasible.

As Britain seeks to function in a more globalised economy, it is imperative not to undertake reforms that reduce productivity levels or encourage capital to move elsewhere. If the net effect of social investment, prevention and pre-distribution is higher labour costs, productivity must increase correspondingly. Measures that raise bottom-end

DOI: 10.1057/9781137328113

wages must be accompanied by a programme to improve the quality of human capital through education, training and investment to upgrade the capacity of industry to utilise a higher quality workforce. The fact that other developed economies in Europe function successfully with rather lower levels of income inequality (Atkinson 2007), demonstrates that this is possible.

The scope for such policies to reduce poverty among the 59 per cent of poor households who contain a working member is unclear. They would be a useful addition alongside the moves to reframe redistributive welfare in terms of child poverty, contribution and responsibility outlined earlier. They would also support the general shift towards policies that promote the perception of those on low incomes as sharing the normal aspirations of the mass of the population for social engagement, family life and productive work that pays enough to achieve it.

Conclusions

The pro-welfare trilemma between inclusiveness, feasibility and effectiveness is most challenging in relation to vertically redistributive policies to address unpopular minority needs. The discussion in this chapter shows that the intransigence of the distinction between deserving and undeserving poor and the disconnection between tax rates and the quality of welfare state services in the public mind can create major difficulties in developing more inclusive and generous policies and financing them. It identifies three broad directions in response: benefits targeted at child poverty, feasible because this group is less likely to be stigmatised; approaches which address the reasons why humane welfare for the most vulnerable attracts relatively little public support and seek to reframe provision in terms of reciprocity, fellow-feeling and responsibility; and those which highlight potential economic advantages from carefully managed social investment, prevention and pre-distribution policies which would also mitigate inequality.

Four broad conclusions emerge: first there are real opportunities to develop new policies that redistribute towards children and reframe public perceptions of claimers not as dependants but as contributors to society taking responsibility for their needs. This approach highlights the extent to which those on benefits share values and aspirations in relation to work and a decent family life with the mass of the population.

DOI: 10.1057/9781137328113

The facts that a majority of poor households contain workers and that substantial numbers of those impoverished are children, who cannot be held responsible for their own poverty, reinforce the political feasibility of such policies. The approach will help mitigate stigma and strengthen support for collective welfare.

Second there are limits to the scope of the policies discussed above. Contributory welfare, highlighting reciprocity, applies best to those of working age and able to make a plausible contribution. Attempts to build empathy are most powerful for poverty among children and low-income families in paid work. It is easier to present those able to make a contribution to society through current or future employment or care as taking responsibility for their lives. The stress on individual values and behaviour works less well in justifying support for some of the most vulnerable groups, who are more marginal in a ruthlessly competitive economy: people with very low levels of skill, those with unstable family lives, street homeless people and those defined as disabled. A contribution-based system could diminish sympathy for a smaller group of very vulnerable people and must be combined with other approaches to welfare.

Third, the costs of such policies are also large. Ending child poverty through redistribution would require perhaps £10bn, with nearly three times as much needed to eliminate poverty among adults. Any feasible strategy must shift towards more redistributive outcomes over time, chipping away at inequalities and building support as the reframing of people's perceptions mitigates social divisions.

New policies to reframe perceptions of claimers and make higher spending on their needs politically acceptable march hand-in-hand with strategies to advance social investment, prevention and pre-distribution. The latter group of policies is essential to reduce inequalities in pay and improve opportunities for women with young children and for those at the bottom over time, so that the costs of redistributive welfare become less onerous and antipathy towards the poor decreases. Social investment and prevention will also involve spending. It is sometimes assumed that pre-distribution, because it rests largely on regulation, is cheap. Effective regulation costs money and the move towards outsourcing increases these costs.

The fourth point is that these policies mark a major change in approaches to poverty and inequality. They require strong political commitment and moral leadership. It is hard to see how more humane

DOI: 10.1057/9781137328113

and inclusive policies can be justified entirely in terms of investment, mobility or enhanced productivity. A feasible political movement must also make the case that more generous and inclusive welfare is good in itself, and that this justifies extra tax and spending.

In Chapter 4 we consider how the constraints of generosity and inclusiveness, feasibility and effectiveness apply to the popular high-spending services less hard hit by current retrenchment but more vulnerable to the longer-term challenges.

DOI: 10.1057/9781137328113

4

Responding to the Trilemma: Affordable Policies to Make Popular Mass Services More Inclusive

Abstract: *The problems in addressing the long-term pressures on popular services for health care, education and pensions at first sight differ from those in ensuring generous and inclusive benefits to reduce inequalities and mitigate poverty among the stigmatised minorities most affected by cutbacks. The amounts required to sustain the popular mass services are large but in fact rather less than the spending increases actually achieved in those areas during the past 30 years. Spending at this level requires political commitment, but is feasible. The real problem for those who want better welfare is to ensure that less advantaged groups get the same outcomes from the services that everyone uses as the more privileged. This requires cutting tax subsidies to private provision, extra spending on the health and education of lower-income groups and better pensions.*

Keywords: access; ageing population; Baumol wage effect; education; equality; health; internal market; NHS; pensions; redistribution; rising aspirations; social care; spending

Taylor-Gooby, Peter. *The Double Crisis of the Welfare State and What We Can Do About It.* Basingstoke: Palgrave Macmillan, 2013. DOI: 10.1057/9781137328113

DOI: 10.1057/9781137328113

There is no doubt that the big-spending social services at the heart of the long-run crisis are highly valued. Health care, education and pensions are far and away the most popular areas for extra state spending in the UK, as elsewhere in Europe (Svallfors 2007). Support for more spending on health has in fact fallen slightly since the early 2000s following a gradual expansion since the early 1990s and more rapid spending increases in the early 2000s, but remains the top priority. Enthusiasm for education spending has been consistently high during the past two decades with a slight downturn following the crisis. Pensions remain a high priority. These services are heavily used by many voters and in the case of the first two employ very large numbers of people at a range of levels. Even when implementing the most severe programme of cuts ever undertaken in this country without the shock of a major war, the government felt it necessary to ring-fence health and education and commit to further expansion of pensions. The previous government encountered very little opposition to its spending increases in these areas and to the extra 1 per cent National Insurance contribution justified as funding higher health spending after the Wanless Review (HM Treasury 2002, chapter 6).

These points suggest that it may be easier to meet the expected long-run pressures (which apply mainly to health, social care and pension spending) and still retain electoral support than to sustain (let alone increase) spending on cheaper vertically redistributive welfare benefits. The studies of cost-effectiveness discussed in Chapter 1 show that stringent attempts to restrain costs have succeeded in slowing but not stopping expansion. The pressures are real but not insuperable given the extended time period over which they apply. OBR's central estimate of the extra resources needed to maintain standards in the UK is some £75bn at current prices by 2062, or 20 per cent of the cost of current pensions, health and social care and education, or 4.5 per cent of GDP (OBR 2012c). The EC Economic and Finance Committee's more detailed analysis leads to a comparable figure: slightly over 4 per cent (EC 2012). The main reason for the lower EC figure is that it includes spending on unemployment, assumed to fall in future years, and estimates wage effects at a rather lower level. OBR goes on to suggest that the burden of higher spending could be spread through cumulative tax increases over the intervening period. In this case the cost works out at about 0.4 per cent GDP for each of the next five decades (OBR 2012c, 14). Projections over so long a period are of course uncertain, but are the best guide we have to how pressures are likely to develop. The case for treating the tax load as manageable can be strengthened by considering four further points.

DOI: 10.1057/9781137328113

First, and perhaps more importantly, the areas under consideration are ones in which people choose to spend more when they are able to do so. Spending on pensions rose from about 6 to about 7 per cent of GDP between 1994 and 2007, between the end of the early 1990s and onset of the 2008–9 recessions. Spending on health care increased rather faster: by 2 per cent of GDP over the 13 years. A slower average rate of increase (allowing for future recessions, when extra spending will be more difficult) over the next half-century will meet the OBR target. The best case for claiming such increases are feasible lies in the fact that they simply follow the long-term trends established during periods of growth: business as usual for the welfare state.

Second, there is further evidence from John Hills' analysis of spending on public and private welfare during the past three decades that people value these services. Even as public welfare spending expanded between 1979–80 and 2007–8, non-state spending in these areas grew even faster. The UK had grown substantially richer over the period. Total spending on health care, education and personal care rose from £75.1bn to £234.5bn at 2008–9 prices. Purely private spending on these services where the provider, the decision to spend and the finance were entirely private increased from 8.4 to 13.7 per cent of the total (calculated from Hills 2011, table 1). Private pension contributions more than doubled during the period (Hills *et al.* 2011, 597), but spending in this area is influenced by tax subsidies, national insurance remission and other state policies and is not counted as purely private for our purposes. The amounts involved are moderate in relation to state spending, an increase of £12.4bn or 0.8 per cent of GDP over 28 years. Some of the extra will cover private cosmetic surgery, classes undertaken as a leisure activity or similar pursuits. Nonetheless that fact that people chose to spend more in these areas alongside expanding state provision shows how much they value health, social care and education and will pay for them. The real choice is between extra spending through an unequal and fragmented but responsive system of private provision or through a more managed and potentially more comprehensive expansion of the welfare state.

Third, the challenges facing the UK in the long term are in no way exceptional. The country stands roughly at the mid-point of the range of European countries ranked by future spending pressures at 4 per cent of GDP, against an EU27 average of 4.5. In the shorter-term, up to 2020, the UK faces no net pressures at all, aided by high immigration and relatively low spending on social provision. In some countries, notably

DOI: 10.1057/9781137328113

the more generous Nordic group and in Belgium and Germany, existing commitments are much more testing. Figure 4.1, calculated from the EC report, shows substantial variations between countries and within groups of countries in anticipated spending during the next half-century. These national variations emerge whether countries are ranked by stage of development, from high to low spenders, or from Nordic citizenship welfare states to the more liberal market-oriented UK and Ireland. The problems faced here emerge elsewhere; many countries face much tougher challenges than does the UK.

The fourth point concerns recent experiences in modifying services to contain costs, first with pensions and then in other areas. Most European countries have embarked on the pension reforms necessary to meet demographic pressures. The changes include raising pension ages, merging different social insurance schemes, making entitlement stricter (although most schemes have also changed their rules to give some entitlement to women and men engaged in caring) and introducing demographic regulators, so that pension levels are cut back as the balance between working and retired population shifts (Arza and Kohli 2007). An EU study concluded that future pension commitments had been reduced by something like a quarter through such measures

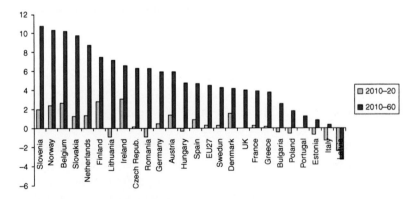

FIGURE 4.1   *Projected changes in age-related expenditure, selected European countries 2010–20 and 2010–60 (per cent GDP)*

Note: The projections include spending on pensions, health, long-term care, education and unemployment and their impact on economic growth. They cover all policy changes announced up to December 2011.

Source: Calculated from EC (2012), Table 1.

DOI: 10.1057/9781137328113

between the mid-1980s and the mid-2000s (EC 2006). In the traditionally high-spending and social democratic Sweden, the 1998 reforms stabilised total pension contributions at about 12 per cent of average lifetime earnings. If the previous scheme had continued they would have risen to about 20 per cent by 2020 (Fenge and Werding 2004) Similarly, most European countries have pursued a range of reforms to health and social care designed to control spending and focus it more accurately on social need (Hassenteufel and Palier 2007, Palier and Martin 2007, Pavolini and Guillen 2013).

The UK has pursued policies which increase state pension levels and are intended to expand enrolment in private schemes, so that people will pay a minimum of 4 per cent of their own incomes (just over 3 per cent after tax relief) into occupational top-up pensions by 2018. Pension age has been increased to 65 for both sexes and will rise to 67 by 2028. Protests have been relatively weak and focused mainly on the fact that women, whose pension age (previously 60) is already in process of being increased to 65 by 2018, face very sharp rises in retirement age. The changes also throw extra pressures on disability benefits for those unable to continue working. The outcome will be a continuing gradual rise in the cost of state pensions but at a rate that can be managed by feasible tax increases.

The UK faces substantial extra costs but these can be met, provided that governments maintain pressures on spending with the same success in slowing the escalation of costs as during the past 15 years and are willing to raise the taxes necessary to finance gradual increases in spending. Effective action requires political leadership to gain support for such policies at an early stage when they will be most effective. A degree of cross-party consensus will be needed to ensure that the programme is maintained over time. This is not a trivial requirement in the UK's party-competitive political system.

If real spending increases that safeguard the popular horizontally redistributive health, education and pension services are achieved, defenders of a humane welfare state face a further challenge: ensuring that the extra spending takes place within a framework of inclusive provision that promotes social cohesion, rather than through mixed private, voluntary and state services with substantial differences in entitlement between different income groups. This involves making the case for a generous and inclusive welfare state.

DOI: 10.1057/9781137328113

Genuinely inclusive provision: the shortcomings of universalism

One aspect of effectiveness is already covered in the above discussion of whether people will accept the spending increases needed to maintain standards in the major horizontally redistributive services. Similar rises are normal in the past development of the UK welfare state: there is no obvious reason why spending increases at these rates cannot be sustained into the future. We now consider effectiveness in relation to the success with which the services meet the positive welfare state goals of inclusiveness and generosity and whether they will nourish support for those objectives among the public. The continued pressures necessary to hold down the rate of spending increase will require the permanent implementation of change at a rate comparable to that of the past two decades, as government continually seeks to ensure that resources are used efficiently. Such a programme will involve winners and losers and may generate tensions. The changes should be designed to enhance, or at least not damage, public support for moves towards more inclusive and generous policies.

The services under consideration are comprehensive in the sense that health care and education are available to all citizens and full pensions to those who have a minimum of 30 years contributions, rising to 35 years in 2017, with contributions credited for parental leave and care for a child, sick, disabled or frail elderly person. The services are also relatively generous in the national but not in an international context. Britain spends more per head on pensions than on benefits for poor people of working age but rather less than do France, Germany and the Nordic countries. Since the services are more or less universal they provide a collective context for people's understanding of their interests and help buttress further moves towards greater solidarity. However there are real limitations to the extent to which current provision promotes inclusiveness.

Titmuss argued that middle-class people were advantaged by tax subsidies for private services in the post-war welfare state through the 'social division of welfare' (1955). Le Grand built on this using survey data to demonstrate that better-off people made most use of the more expensive aspects of health, education, transport, housing and social care (1982). A large number of subsequent studies show that, even in the case of universal provision, both access to the services and outcomes for

DOI: 10.1057/9781137328113

users are unequal, by social class, income group, region, gender and in many cases ethnicity.

Health care: The authoritative Marmot Review (2010), following on from the Townsend (1982), Acheson (1998) and Black Reports (1980), presses home the point that universal provision has raised overall standards, but has had limited impact on inequalities in health. Life expectancy, infant mortality, long-term illnesses that circumscribe people's lives, the incidence of major diseases, including circulatory disease and cancer (2010, 45), and mental health problems all vary between women and men and between social classes, income groups, regions of the country and areas ranked by level of deprivation (2010, chapter 2). For example, life expectancy at birth for women was 85 for higher professional and managerial workers (class I), but only 78 among unskilled workers (class V: 2010, figure 2.1). Among men, corresponding statistics are 85 and 77. Although health has generally improved over time, there is no indication of a decline in inequality, rather the reverse. The improvement for women was seven percentage points in class I and only five points in class V between the mid-1970s and the early 2000s. For men the figures are eight points for class I and six for class V.

The scale of inequalities and their resistance to change leads Marmot to recommend a comprehensive strategy, touching most areas of people's lives. This includes action focused on early childhood, on parenting, on public health issues, on health behaviour in areas like smoking, alcohol consumption and exercise and on environment in the workplace, home and school. This emphasis on a positive health strategy that extends far beyond the curative and health maintenance services (to which the bulk of NHS spending is directed) raises a dilemma for reformers. The existing system is highly popular, valued and trusted. Many changes, including those designed to improve the efficiency of resource-utilisation, for example, hospital mergers, are strongly resisted. Moving beyond a curative strategy may appear promising in terms of the goal of greater social equality in health outcomes. It may be less popular with the electorate as a policy direction if it involves switching resources from the existing pattern of NHS spending.

Non-state health care makes up about 18 per cent of all health spending in the UK in 2008, a substantial sum, in view of the fact that state spending accounts for about 7.5 per cent of GDP, about £120bn. Private medical care is about three-fifths out-of-pocket expenditure on drugs, equipment and procedures, with the rest split equally between

DOI: 10.1057/9781137328113

commercial medical insurance and not-for-profit agencies (OECD 2012a). Most medical insurance in the UK is provided through employment, mainly for middle-class employees, whether employer subsidised or as group schemes. It is assumed (in the absence of hard national evidence) that out-of-pocket purchase of one-off procedures is mainly by better-off people, in view of the cost. To what extent use of the private sector leads to major inequalities in outcomes, as opposed to faster, more comfortable access to routine treatment, is hard to estimate. The existence of private medicine is likely to lead to divergent interests for the procedures for which it is widely available, mainly elective surgery with relatively predictable outcomes.

Education: The National Equalities Panel report (NEP 2010, chapter 3) summarises available data. There are substantial differences in outcomes in schools and to an even greater extent among the adult population. Gender, ethnicity, region and poverty, measured by receipt of free school meals, also make a difference, and the pattern has changed over time. The top 10 per cent of girls are about five points ahead of the top 10 per cent of boys in overall performance. At the bottom, the lowest tenth of boys fall about six percentage points below the lowest tenth of girls (NEP 2010, 71–2). In terms of qualifications among the working population, and particularly among older age-groups, the balance is reversed. About 28 per cent of men aged 50 have an A-level or equivalent, but only 18 per cent of women have similar qualifications. In contrast to the younger cohort, fewer women than men in this age-group have degrees or higher qualifications and more have their highest qualification at GCSE or below (NEP 2010, figure 3.7).

Educational attainment is closely linked to income. 'Working-age adults with no educational qualification were about twice as likely to live in low-income households as those with a qualification below degree level' (DWP 2012c, 148). A large number of studies indicate that more middle-class and better-off parents are able to gain advantage for their children by using their cultural capital and resources to locate the best schools, train their children for access and negotiate entry procedures, transport children and buy houses near prestigious schools, so that class advantage persists despite a universal right to schooling (Ball 2008, Gewirtz *et al.* 1995, Burgess *et al.* 2006, 14, Leech and Campos 2003).

The existence of private schools skews inequalities further. As Hills points out, 'the private school population comes not just from more affluent households, but also disproportionately from particular ethnic

DOI: 10.1057/9781137328113

groups' (NEP 2010, 14). Only 7 per cent of secondary school students are in the private sector in England and Wales, but about half this group performed at a level equivalent to the top 20 per cent of state school students in 2008 and about 30 per cent equivalent to the top 10 per cent in state schools. Data to provide a compelling answer to the question of whether it is the exclusivity and extra resources in private schooling that confers advantage on those who can afford to pay substantial fees (widely believed, including by those who actually pay the fees) or whether the association between private schooling and access to prestigious universities and positions in the labour market reflects the intrinsic quality of the students are not available. A study in the later 1990s showed that private school students at Oxford and Cambridge gain rather lower degree results than state school students who enter with the same qualifications. This suggests that the private school cohort gain the same A-levels as those at state schools at rather lower levels of ability (Smith and Naylor 2001). In other words, private school students are buying privileged access. Whether or not this interpretation is correct, the association between private schooling and privileged outcomes in later employment, initially demonstrated in the Donnison report (1970), persists.

Persisting inequalities within education, the evidence of class advantage within a universal system and the erosive effects on shared interests of the private sector pose difficult questions for those committed to greater inclusiveness. Substantial interests among parents with access to more privileged schools, professional groups, the schools themselves and now the more fragmented range of providers are likely to oppose change. Equally the processes that confer privilege on one group create less privileged groups within the system who may be mobilised.

Pensions: Inequality at the bottom end has steadily declined. The proportion falling below the 60 per cent poverty line after housing costs roughly halved from 29 per cent in 1979 to 14 per cent in 2010–11. This is a very different pattern from that of working-age adults where the proportion below the poverty line has fluctuated between 19 and 22 per cent since 1991–2, with increases anticipated (DWP 2012c, table 5.1tr). Real increases in pension rates and the increasing maturity of occupational pension schemes are mainly responsible for the improvement. The proportion of pensioners in poverty is currently 30 per cent among those without occupational pensions, but only 8 per cent among those who have them (DWP 2012c, chart 6.1). For material deprivation (unable to afford at least one of 15 items of basic household use) the corresponding

DOI: 10.1057/9781137328113

figures are 20 and 5 per cent. There have been real advances towards greater inclusiveness at the bottom end. The decision to uprate pensions generously, so that a greater proportion of national spending over time will go to pensioners, increasing by about a half in real term from £80bn to something like £125bn between 2012 and 2062 and approaching spending on health care, will advance this (Figure 4.2). Set against this, the increase in the pension age to 67 will penalise those, mainly already on lower incomes, whose earnings decline in late middle age or who are vulnerable to work-related disabilities.

The state pension system includes a low basic flat-rate national insurance pension, an earnings-related second pension and a means-tested pension designed to bring pensioner incomes above the poverty line. New policies will bring these together for most pensioners into a simpler flat-rate pension from 2017. Occupational pensions compound inequality, but pensioner incomes are less unequal than those of the working population. The top decile of women pensioners receive some five times as much as the bottom decile, substantially less than the ratio for women of mature working age (45–60) which is about 12 to 1 (NEP 2010, table 6.2). Corresponding figures for men are 3.5 to 1 for pensioners and 8 to 1 for mature working age. There are substantial inequalities in the

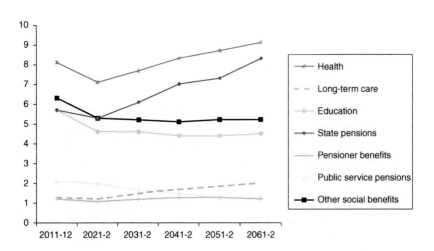

FIGURE 4.2   *Projected social spending, 2011–12 to 2061–2 (per cent GDP)*
Source: Calculated from OBR (2012c), table 3.6.

DOI: 10.1057/9781137328113

incomes of disabled and non-disabled pensioners but these are smaller than those among the working-age population (table 6.4). There are also substantial differences among minority ethnic groups. Most experience much higher inequalities than the majority population (table 6.3). The fact that income divisions between social groups are rather narrower in old age may help promote solidarity among this group, although ideas may be more strongly influenced by people's experience during their working lives.

The challenge of developing the mass services to promote inclusiveness is made more difficult by the fact that the universality of provision is now under threat. As Chapter 1 showed, current policies tend to fragment state services, weakening their capacity to underpin collective support, and extend private provision. One possibility is that people will behave more as consumers, in competition with other service users. Their concerns will focus increasingly on specific mainly commercial providers and on the choice between them, rather than on the collective responsibilities of government. In any case the changes will make the regulatory task of establishing whether common standards are met and of enforcing them more difficult.

We now go on to consider the policy directions that might prove feasible and effective in addressing long-term pressures on the welfare state, and in moving welfare attitudes towards greater generosity and inclusion.

Feasible and effective policies in health care, education and pensions

The above discussion suggests that sufficient resources can be gained through the existing system to ensure the sustainability of popular mass services. Real issues of equality and inclusion dog existing provision in these areas, despite the universal reach of education, health care and pensions. These problems will to grow more intransigent as a result of cutbacks and current restructuring. New policy directions focus on three main objectives: greater equality and inclusion, responsiveness to the demands of service users and rigorous spending controls.

Different considerations apply to the human services (health and social care and education) from pensions and we consider them separately.

DOI: 10.1057/9781137328113

Equality and inclusion: The above discussion points out the importance of the interests already entrenched to defend inequalities within existing education and health care systems, currently being joined by a much-strengthened and increasingly international commercial private sector. Resources are constrained so that major increases in spending across the board in addition to those needed to meet the longer-term pressures are unlikely to be sustainable. This suggests that a careful combination of targeting extra resources on those at the bottom, improving services for the mass of the population and seeking to restrain the exercise of privilege through regulation and legislation is most likely to be viable.

There is considerable experience with targeted approaches in education and health care during the period from 2001 to 2010. These included area based policies (Education Action Zones and the Excellence in Cities initiatives in education and Health Action Zones which provided extra resources and support to the most deprived fifth of local authorities and primary care trusts) and a range of targeted grants and interventions, most notably premia for local education authorities for those on free school meals now rolled into the rather smaller pupil premium. Extra health care resources were also targeted nationally to improve standards in care for major health problems, including cancer and circulatory disease.

These programmes have had some effect. Chapter 3 discussed the sharp and cost-effective improvements in examination results obtained for relatively small investments over a small number of years in carefully designed targeted programmes in the early 2000s. Other targeted initiatives in education include the means-tested Educational Maintenance Allowance for 16–19 year olds, which improved participation by about 12 per cent (Lupton *et al.* 2009, 82, Bolton 2011, 9). For younger children the National Childcare Strategy, combined with Childcare Tax Credit, extension of education plus day-care through primary schooling (now expanded to an entry age of three for part-time schooling and two for disadvantaged children by the current government) and the Sure Start nursery programme embodied a combination of more universal services with targeting to make sure that lower-income people got better access and help with costs. These policies provided extra resources for all parents, but targeted lower-income and deprived children. Resources for under-fives more than doubled from 0.21 to 0.47 per cent of GDP between 1997–98 and 2006–7 (Stewart 2009, table 3.1).

In health care, the reforms achieved some reduction in health inequalities between the 'Spearhead' areas (the fifth of local authority areas with

DOI: 10.1057/9781137328113

the worst health and social deprivation nationally) and the population as a whole. For example the gap in mortality from heart disease fell from 37 to 23 per cent between 1995–7 and 2006–8, and from 21 to 18 per cent for cancer. However other gaps, for infant mortality and between women and men actually increased (DH 2009, Sassi 2009, 145–9). Outcomes varied substantially between individual areas in ways that are hard to explain (King's Fund 2011). These developments took place in the context of rapid improvements in access and falls in overall waiting times achieved by extra resources.

These experiences suggest ways forward that combine the targeting and social investment discussed in Chapter 3 with an improvement in overall standards into a more effective universalism that can retain mass support. They also indicate that inequalities are stubborn and not all initiatives will succeed.

Further feasible reforms might seek to restrict some of the advantages of more privileged groups in relation to access to the most valuable areas within state provision. In education this would include stricter regulation to limit the capacity of high demand schools to manage admissions in a way which gears up the advantage of more middle-class students. A thorough-going equal access policy would involve free student transport over relatively long distances as areas of residence become more segregated. Similar logics would allocate substantial extra resources to more deprived areas in health care but operate through funding premia within the existing health care system, monitored to ensure that they were deployed as envisaged, to maintain inclusion and promote greater use of the services by lower-income people. Other practicable policies include equalisation of funding for over 16s between schools, sixth-form colleges and Further Education colleges. These colleges tend to teach a higher proportion of working class students, to cover less academic courses and receive fewer resources. Funding allocations for 2011–12 work out at £5344 per head in schools, £4402 in colleges and £3474 for apprenticeships (YPLA 2010, 4–5).

Regulation could also be extended to manage private providers who gain tax advantages through charitable status: most private schools and some health care organisations. This would involve stricter insistence that the resources provided are available to and are actually used by all citizens, and not restricted by the ability to pay or attractiveness to the provider, so that they do not become an avenue to privilege. The attempt by the Charity Commission from 2008 to encourage private schools to

DOI: 10.1057/9781137328113

widen use of their resources had some partial success but encountered serious opposition (since it threatens the schools' exclusivity which is a major selling point) and has been much diluted after a legal ruling (BBC 2011). This turned on whether providing education in itself fulfils the requirements for charitable status or whether the impact on provision across the community of a separate system directed mainly at a better-off minority was relevant. A government with a strong mandate could clarify charity law to ensure that resources were opened to wider community use. The same principle could also be applied across health care, to ensure that health insurance providers as registered charities did not direct their benefits to specific social groups, discriminating through fees.

Further development of a more inclusive universalism might extend the remit of health care and education in ways that apply to the whole population but are of specific benefit to disadvantaged groups. The preventive and early detection strategies advocated by Marmot (2010) seek to influence diet, exercise, alcohol intake and smoking. These can be applied nationally. The evidence discussed in Chapter 3 indicates that they will be of most benefit to those groups whose health improved least as a result of the injection of more money overall into the NHS during the past 25 years. The move towards greater involvement in learning through the life-course advantages the groups who succeed less well in the labour market. For example, a study by Blanden and colleagues covering 2000 to 2005 shows that the return to women workers (approaching 10 per cent in enhanced lifetime income) from time spent in earning qualifications after schooling is very much higher than that to men (1 or 2 per cent: Blanden *et al.* 2012, 501).

Inequalities in pensions can also be addressed in an inclusive way through reforms directed at low-income people and at provision as a whole, together with regulation for privileged groups. Targeted support to lift pensioners above the poverty line through means-tested pension supplements has been in place since 1948. It played a major role in the halving of pensioner poverty outlined above. The rate of increase of state pension is now pegged to the retail price index, the earnings index or set at 2.5 per cent, whichever is highest. This will result in real gains for pensioners and can be seen as strengthening cohesion, but is expensive and likely to widen the gap between this group and people of working age on benefits even further. The decision to raise the pension age reflects overall improvements in health and life expectancy but will impact

DOI: 10.1057/9781137328113

differentially on lower social groups who experience most disability in late middle age. An expansion of disability benefits will be required to address needs among this group.

Spending on targeted universalism will require real tax increases. One obvious candidate for realising extra resources is the tax subsidy to middle-class private pension contributions (£17.1bn or 1.1 per cent of GDP for 2010–11) with an extra £6.8bn relief for the investment income of pension funds (HMRC 2012, table Pen6). Possible further measures include limiting tax relief to the standard tax rate or reducing tax relief on investment growth. Smaller sums (perhaps £1bn) would be available, at the cost of targeting benefits that are currently universal, by restricting the winter fuel allowance and pensioners' free bus travel to lower-income groups.

This discussion shows that a combination of policies directed at the most disadvantaged groups and, at the same time, at the mass of the population is possible in health, education and pensions. Such policies could improve equality while retaining social cohesion and commitment from the electorate. Equality could be promoted further by strengthening state regulatory powers to reduce the capacity of better-off groups to maintain their privileges through the use of exclusive private services, and by restricting regressive subsidies through tax relief. Since these policies target resources on specific groups or address their goals through regulation rather than direct spending, the costs are real but not on the scale of those necessary to meet the longer-term challenge in this area. One source for the finance is the tax subsidies mentioned above.

Responsiveness to service users: Responsiveness to the needs and demands of service users is valued for three reasons: first it is part of the valuing of individuals and their dignity that is at the basis of any humane programme for the welfare state. Second, the perception that the social services take people's individual needs seriously is also essential to public confidence and to the success of future demands for extra taxation to sustain them. Third, there is good evidence that internal markets in which service users are able to express their needs can be effective in combining cost-efficiency and service quality. Unfortunately there are also indications that the perception that cost-efficiency predominates can contradict the perception that users are valued as individuals, so that trust in the commitment of providers to the needs of users is undermined.

Debates about responsiveness have centred chiefly on the use of competitive markets, typically as part of a new public management programme (Flynn 2007) and, more recently, on personalisation or personal budgeting. Collective democratic solutions have received little attention in social policy.

Internal market reforms require the different agencies providing the service, for example, various clinics, GP practices, hospitals, care homes or domiciliary services in health and social care, or schools and colleges in education, to compete to attract users. Money follows the service user, so that success in the market directly influences the budget. The government department responsible sets, monitors and enforces standards. A major issue is whether and under what conditions non-state commercial or third sector suppliers enter the market.

There is considerable experience of these systems as they have evolved since the late 1980s in health and social care and education, and more recently across a wide range of state services. This points to four conclusions.

First, internal markets have had considerable success in combining cost-efficiency with innovation, attested by the speed with which they have been adopted in many developed countries (OECD 2011b, Béland and Gran 2008, chapter 1). Second, the impact on standards depends on the detail of the contracts, monitoring and control (Le Grand 2003, chapters 7 and 8). As already pointed out competition solely on price may drive down standards (Gaynor and Town 2012). The prioritisation of particular targets may damage standards in other areas of the service (Bevan and Hood 2006). The risk that providing agencies will pick the easiest cases is a constant challenge (Bartlett *et al.* 1998, see Wilson 2010 for a review). Nonetheless, there is good evidence from natural experiments that compare England with Wales, Scotland and Northern Ireland (which have similar funding levels in health and social care but have not moved so far towards the new approach) and from other sources that market competition can be a powerful tool in maintain quality and controlling costs when it is effectively managed (Propper *et al.* 2008, Le Grand 2007).

Third, the approach is, unsurprisingly, most effective where the objective and the associated incentive structure are simple and transparent, and when there is a clear consensus on the priority of various activities (Wilson 2010). This raises issues in health care and education, where services are complex, the outcomes that can be prioritised are numerous and sometimes conflicting, and there is controversy over the best way to meet them.

DOI: 10.1057/9781137328113

Fourth, outcomes in relation to responsiveness are more equivocal. Internal markets typically succeed in providing services that respond to demand at least as well as alternative systems. The period during which the internal market in health care was rolled out was the longest period of sustained rise in public satisfaction with the service during the past three decades. The percentage of those interviewed by the British Social Attitudes survey who said they were very satisfied or satisfied with the NHS, which had fluctuated between the high 30s and the high 40s between the mid-1980s and 2000, rose steadily from 40 to 71 per cent between 2000 and 2010 (King's Fund 2012). It then fell abruptly to 58 per cent in 2011. One year's results are not conclusive but there is evidence from the responses of those with recent experience of the service and from surveys by other agencies that the fall is due to a perceived decline in quality of service, perhaps resulting from spending constraint. This fits with the evidence that most people appear to value objective standards in services such as health care much more highly than they do responsiveness to user demands (Appleby and Alvarez-Rosette 2005). There is some evidence of a decline in public trust as users see providers as driven to manage cases within a restricted budget rather than by commitment to care and individual need (Hoggett *et al.* 2006, Taylor-Gooby 2009, chapter 9, Curtice and Heath 2009).

These arguments suggest that internal markets have real value but perhaps more in relation to cost-efficiency than in the public confidence that will help guarantee future public support for extra spending. A different approach to responsiveness is provided through the personalisation of services. In this approach, used most widely in social care but now being introduced in DWP services for disabled people and more broadly in health care, a proportion of the budget spent on the individual is put at the disposal of the service user. Individuals may choose to purchase services from the existing agency, from non-state suppliers, from relatives or from other sources, within guidelines. While it is difficult to assess an innovative approach at an early stage, initial Department of Health studies indicate high levels of satisfaction among most users of personalised budgets (Glendinning *et al.* 2009, Glasby and Littlechild 2009). However satisfaction is much lower among some groups, particularly those with mental health difficulties who have more complex needs that they find harder to predict, and among very old people who may find choice onerous (Glendinning *et al.* 2009, SCIE 2009, 2011). This raises the question of how far personalised budgeting can be taken in areas where most

DOI: 10.1057/9781137328113

people are uncertain as to the service mix that will best address their needs, such as medical care. There is also a persistent concern that the opportunity to supplement state provision from individual resources invites a gradual reduction in funding leading to a decline in overall standards and increased inequalities in outcomes. Personalisation can go some way to advance responsiveness for specific groups and services, but again budgetary issues are important, and the approach cannot be a complete solution.

A further approach to ensuring state services are more responsive, expanding collective democratic rather than individual service user control, has received little attention in social policy but been extensively discussed by political scientists. There are a number of experiments in which budgets for local services have been allocated by neighbourhood committees with considerable success in terms of satisfaction and standards. The best known is the participatory budgeting programme in Porto Alegre in Brazil (Baiocchi 2001, 43, 64). In other cases direct local democracy has been less successful, as particular groups have captured the relevant committees (Morrison and Singer 2007), conflicts over policy directions have hindered progress (Aylett 2010, Harbers 2007) or adequate popular engagement has not been achieved (Ranson *et al.* 2003, 727). Other experiments concern a wide range of activities from consultation and engagement exercises to involvement in policymaking through lay representation, referenda, citizen's juries, crowdsourcing and deliberative polling intended to allow ordinary people greater direct influence over policy outcomes (see Stewart 2007 for an overview).

The original nineteenth century development of municipal selfgovernment in the UK involved a degree of local democracy through an elected authority (Sheldrake 1989) but direct democratic control by local communities has not been prominent in recent social provision, despite some experiments, again mainly by local government (Pratchett *et al.* 2009). The method has attractions in terms of transparent responsiveness but might also generate problems of ensuring equality between areas and co-ordinating services nationally. Greater involvement of residents' groups in the management of local services such as education, health and social care, and possibly experiments in collective control of budgets within a national representative framework, might help in the development of a more effective and engaging democratic process (Stoker 2006, chapter 11).

DOI: 10.1057/9781137328113

Holding down costs and regulating standards: Policy-makers have gained considerable experience in implementing policies to hold down costs during the past three decades, especially in the area of human services. There are strong inbuilt pressures for spending to rise from the relative wage effect discussed in Chapter 2, from the desire of managers to expand their area of authority (Niskanen 1994) and from politicians who gain votes by spending in popular areas (Pierson 1994). Equally, real cost-efficiencies can be obtained in social provision: for most of the period since detailed studies started in the mid-1990s productivity has in fact kept pace with population ageing and rising wage costs in education and health care.

Current policies anticipate considerable savings from the use of private commercial contractors in areas ranging from local government back office services to the allocation of Universal Credit and from disability assessment to managing prisons. Good evidence on the impact of recent privatisation and outsourcing policies is not yet available. It is unclear whether permanent savings will be achieved, despite the claims of a Department for Business, Innovation and Skills review that cost reductions of between 10 and 30 per cent could be expected (Julius 2008, ii). Most of the savings in contracting out to the private sector appear to result from cuts in staffing levels and conditions so that the cost reductions achieved are one-off economies. The competitive outsourcing model also generates other problems to do with fragmentation and effective monitoring.

Most experts believe that the challenge of achieving savings in the health service while confronting demographic pressure requires fundamental re-organisation and greater integration, especially with social care. For example: 'the evidence...is unambiguous. The Nicholson Challenge can only be achieved by making fundamental changes to the way care is delivered... health and social care must be seen as two aspects of the same service and planned together in every area for there to be any chance of a high quality and efficient service being provided which meets the needs of the local population within the funding available' (HC Health Committee, 2012, paras 1, 2). However 'the separate governance and funding systems make full-scale integration a challenging prospect'. Pursuit of short-term savings through contracts with a number of competing providers compounds the problem. The committee goes on to detail the way in which the cutbacks hamper the formation of a long-term strategy. Outsourcing makes effective co-ordination much harder.

DOI: 10.1057/9781137328113

Perhaps more importantly, there appear to be major problems in ensuring that standards can be maintained when competition is mainly on price, the number of competent suppliers is relatively small, state services need to secure continuity of provision and Departments are under pressure to privatise services quickly. In relation to the NHS, a Public Accounts Committee report points out that 'the Department could not provide adequate reassurances that financial problems would not damage either the quality of care or equality of access to all citizens, wherever they live' (HCPAC 2012b, Summary). The chief monitoring agency for hospitals, care homes and care services, the Care Quality Commission, has experienced difficulty in undertaking thorough inspections. It completed only 47 per cent of the intended number in the six months preceding a National Audit Office review in 2011. Its work is 'constrained by gaps in data' and it is unable to keep to its time-table in registering GP practices, care homes, domiciliary services and other providers (NAO 2011, 8, 9). By 2012 it was able to produce its first comprehensive report across NHS and private health and social care. The report expresses concern about the impact of population ageing and resource pressures on standards. It showed that between 80 and 90 per cent of providers performed well in relation to 16 overall measures, an acceptable but not outstanding record. However in some areas standards were much lower. For people with a learning disability, only 71 per cent of NHS providers and 49 per cent of private providers met the care and welfare standards (CQC 2012, 6–10). For private nursing homes only 72 per cent provided effective care (90–2).

The difficulties government encounters in managing large private providers in services for vulnerable people are further illustrated by the abrupt collapse of Southern Cross, a leading supplier of social care homes with about 750 homes and 31,000 residents (about 7 per cent of the total), in June 2011. This resulted from the risks involved in complex sale and lease-back arrangements. A deal involving the transfer of homes to new operators was brokered by the company and by central and local government. This made it possible for care to continue, but at the cost of considerable uncertainty for vulnerable people (SCIE 2011). A House of Commons Public Accounts Committee enquiry concluded that DH had failed to make arrangements to cope with the collapse of a major provider or even monitor the financial health of contractors (HCPAC 2011b).

Problems of regulation and monitoring also apply in outsourcing the management of cash benefits. The National Audit Office report on DWP's relationship with the preferred contractor in assessment of disability benefit entitlement concluded that 'Atos Healthcare has not routinely met all the service standards specified in the contract' (NAO 2012, 6). It noted that the department had failed to seek 'adequate financial redress for underperformance', and pointed out that 38 per cent of Atos assessments were overturned on appeal. DWP later contracted with Atos to manage the main benefit for disabled people judged able to undertake paid work (the Personal Independence Payment) for five years from April 2013.

Monitoring contract compliance imposes further pressures on government. A particularly striking case concerns fraud by employees of A4E, one of the largest providers in the DWP Employment Programme. Newspaper enquiries into the firm's activities to help unemployed people into jobs led to allegations of fraud from 2009 onwards (Observer 2009), resulting in a police investigation in 2012 and demands by MPs for an audit. Contracts with the company were terminated in April 2012 (DWP 2012e). The Public Accounts Committee pointed to a failure to audit and manage contractors and to even define 'what standards a company must meet to be a "fit and proper" organisation with which the Department is willing to contract' (HCPAC 2012a).

More broadly, the Audit Commission argues in favour of greater competition in local government but points out that councils often lack the capacity to manage markets effectively. They employ too few staff with relevant skills and good information on local markets and opportunities (2007). The Public Administration Select Committee inquiry into the 'Big Society' examined outsourcing in general. It concludes:

> the ambition to open up public services to new providers has prompted concerns about the role of private companies which have not thus far been adequately addressed by Ministers. We have recommended greater clarity on the roles of charitable, private and public providers of public services. We also press the Government to outline how crucial issues of accountability in terms of quality and regulatory powers will be managed in the Big Society project, and in particular accountability for public expenditure. (HCPASC 2011, Summary)

Outside the area of social provision, the recent scandals involving the failure of the G4S contract for security for the 2012 London Olympics (G4S 2012) and rate manipulation in the gas (Ofgem 2012) and interbank lending (Thompson and Jones 2012) wholesale markets illustrate the difficulties governments face in regulating relationships with large private agencies.

DOI: 10.1057/9781137328113

Technical interventions have proved reasonably effective in areas where the state can gather good information and exert some control over behaviour. An example is the assessment by NICE of the cost-effectiveness of drug therapies and other approaches in the health service and in social care in order to advise on what should be included on the list of treatments funded by the NHS. While some NICE decisions have been overturned by organised pressure and there are concerns about the quality of some of the evidence presented to the committee (Goldacre 2012, 6, 27–8), the procedures have been effective in restraining prices in most cases and enabling a unified health service to use its bargaining power effectively. This indicates that regulation of markets is possible, provided that government has good information, effective control over spending decisions and is prepared to use its powers. However, the more complex regulatory problems involved in managing contracts with large private organisations where the costs to government of abandoning the supplier are large have given rise to serious difficulties as illustrated above.

The use of markets appears to have real advantages in cost-efficiency and responsiveness. Outsourcing to the private sector carries large risks, particularly when the over-riding concern is to cut costs in the short term, and competition is on price rather than quality. One solution is to move towards carefully monitored internal markets in areas like health care and education, while retaining the capacity to take services provided by unsuccessful agencies back into direct management. Similarly the plausible threat of private competition may be helpful in driving innovation within a state sector internal market. This was previously achieved in the NHS by setting an upper limit of 15 per cent to the proportion of revenue a hospital trust could source from private contracts.

Conclusions

Discussion of generosity and inclusiveness, feasibility and effectiveness in reform shows that there are real possibilities for managing the long-term pressures faced by government in the more popular (and expensive) areas of the welfare state so that sufficient resources can be made available to sustain standards. Problems arise in addressing the inequalities between social groups in access to and outcomes from the services as they are currently structured. The main directions in policy debate follow a more inclusive comprehensive model, combining targeting on

DOI: 10.1057/9781137328113

the least advantaged groups with strong universal provision. They also point to the value of competitive market models and other innovations to control costs within a largely state model of provision. Such policies appear feasible because the services involved are highly valued. People have been willing to accept real increases in spending to sustain them during the past two decades and there is no reason to believe that, when real growth returns, they will not be willing to fund further increases. This approach will require continued pressure to ensure that high levels of cost-efficiency are maintained. More effective universalism can be reinforced through regulatory policies that limit the access of privileged groups to better schools, hospitals and specialists, ensure that private charitable suppliers do not operate policies that exclude lower-income people and curtail subsidies to the middle-class welfare state through tax reliefs in such areas as occupational pensions.

The problems in delivering high standards in a way that promotes universalism and inclusiveness in these services are less severe that those faced in relation to the much less highly regarded welfare services and benefits that redistribute to those on low incomes. They are nonetheless real and will require political leadership to mobilise support for the tax rises necessary to fund the services. Outsourcing compounds the problems of regulation that already face government in relation to the activities of private and charitable agencies in health care and education. Recent experience demonstrates the difficulties confronting central and local government in monitoring standards among private contractors and in enforcing adequate levels of service. These problems are exacerbated by attempts to extend contracting to complex areas of provision with multiple outcomes and difficulties in establishing priorities between them.

For these reasons the most feasible way of promoting greater equality within the mass services of the welfare state appears to be through the use of internal markets, with the presence of non-state providers kept at a minimum level. Such an approach also allows government to inject extra resources in targeted programmes to raise standards for those groups currently least well served within a universalist system. Any move to make these services more generous and inclusive will require extra resources, in addition to those required to meet the long-term pressures, to improve provision for specific groups and to monitor and regulate service agencies more effectively. Even with the extra spending envisaged above, many areas of social provision face the 'permanent austerity' that

DOI: 10.1057/9781137328113

Pierson identified (2001, 456) as necessary to contain rising spending. A redirection towards more generous and inclusive provision for those groups currently least well served might ensure that such a future is not entirely bleak.

In the final chapter we review the argument so far and summarise approaches which may offer a humane, generous, inclusive and feasible response to the double crisis of the welfare state. We then consider how political support for these policies might be mobilised, so that an inclusive and generous welfare state that is effective in meeting the challenges that undoubtedly confront it might gain sufficient stable political support to be a feasible objective for policy-makers.

DOI: 10.1057/9781137328113

5
Making Generous and Inclusive Policies Politically Feasible

Abstract: *Those committed to a more generous and inclusive welfare state face a trilemma in devising policies to meet the double crisis: higher taxes are disliked, the poor are viewed with suspicion and effective, inclusive services demand higher spending. Mass services (NHS, education, pensions) are popular; benefits for the poor are not. Reforms which focus on child poverty, contributory welfare and poverty-level wages are more likely to be politically acceptable. Greater insecurity in a more flexible labour market and pressure for child and elder care and training and work-place rights to help cope with new social risks encourage support for better and more redistributive welfare. More accessible childcare and a better-trained workforce can improve productivity. An inclusive, humane and generous welfare state is feasible, politically and economically. It requires commitment and political leadership.*

Keywords: family; new social risks; social inclusion; state spending; universalism; welfare state trilemma; women

Taylor-Gooby, Peter. *The Double Crisis of the Welfare State and What We Can Do About It.* Basingstoke: Palgrave Macmillan, 2013. DOI: 10.1057/9781137328113

DOI: 10.1057/9781137328113

The double crisis

A crisis is a turning point, a decisive moment when previous arrangements break down and a new pathway for social development must be found. Chapter 1 reviewed the two crisis trends driving major structural reforms in the UK welfare state: immediate and long-term.

The 2007 banking crisis led to economic crisis, fiscal crisis and a series of recessions from 2008 onwards. The severity of the problems for state welfare results from government decisions to prioritise deficit reduction, balance the budget mainly by cutting spending rather than by raising taxes and impose the most stringent cuts on low-income households and the more deprived regions. Provision for the mass of the population, which accounts for many more resources, is less harshly affected. The problems for the welfare state are compounded by a programme of restructuring for virtually all state services in a way that fragments provision, massively expands the role of the for-profit private sector and tightens work incentives further.

Capitalism is a flexible and intensely dynamic economic system that has sustained high rates of economic growth and improved living standards across the planet. It is also unstable, prone to a cyclical alternation of vigour and stagnation and to occasional recession. As Schumpeter pointed out, drawing on Marx's application of Hegelian dialectic to social and economic development, 'creative destruction' lies at its heart (1942). The depth of the recessions starting in 2008 reflects the greater interconnectedness of global systems, particularly in banking, and the lack of a forceful and co-ordinated reflationary response after 2010 (Gamble 2011). The specific difficulties of the UK stem from its exceptional reliance on the financial sector, in which activity tends to exaggerate peaks and troughs in the material economy, and the decision to curtail state spending and investment at a rate not seen since the early 1920s (Gough 2011a). One element in the commitment to much harsher spending cuts than in comparable countries and to a root-and-branch restructuring of virtually all public services may be a determination to impose a new radical liberal direction on the British political economy.

The new programme exacerbates the existing cleavage between services and benefits for the mass of the population (health care, education and pensions) and those targeted on poor minorities (tax credits, housing benefits, unemployment benefits, lone parent benefits). It builds on

DOI: 10.1057/9781137328113

already deepening divisions between better- and worse-off groups in income, life-chances and area of residence and harsher stigmatisation of the poor of working age. The pressures on government spending are real. Social divisions are deeper than in the major European countries. The immediate crisis in the UK is sharpened by the decision to use the opportunity to cut back provisions for the poor and to break up existing collective institutions in health care, education and the other major state services.

The longer-run crisis for the welfare state also follows from pressures which, like the 2007 recession, affect almost all developed countries. In this case, the main issues are population ageing, rising real wage costs in human services and the aspirations of many service users. Ageing impacts mainly on demand for health and social care and pensions, wage costs chiefly affect education, health and social care, and rising aspirations apply to most areas of provision, particularly pension spending and standards in health, social care and education. The pressures in the UK are in fact less intense than those in comparable European countries, since demographic shifts are more gradual, anticipated high rates of immigration mitigate wage pressures and spending levels are rather lower in the first place.

Experience since the mid-1990s indicates that rising wage costs can be contained through vigorous effort. It is simply unclear what impact the reform programme, involving extensive outsourcing in health and social care, the introduction of new techniques such as payment by results and social bonds, the fragmentation of the schooling and health care systems and the termination of state funding for students and university teaching, will have on long-term future developments. Whatever the impact on cost-efficiency, there are indications that the new more complex systems will be much more difficult to regulate than previous ones. If quality falls, outcomes will run counter to aspirations and support for the services will be eroded. This increases the pressure on government to monitor provision effectively and to find ways of reintegrating services. If demand rises at the rate anticipated by the OBR and the European Commission and public support remains high, the extra spending, perhaps an extra 0.4 per cent of an expanding GDP each decade for 50 years, appears feasible.

The long-run and immediate crises are linked by the fact that both bear most heavily on provision for the poor. The greater popularity of the expensive and horizontally distributive services most affected

DOI: 10.1057/9781137328113

by the long-run pressures generates a demand to transfer resources from the welfare state for the poor to bolster provision in these areas; similarly the stigmatisation and social segregation of low-income minorities leads a government committed to cutbacks to cut spending on these groups most harshly. Any effective response to the pressures on a humane and inclusive welfare state needs also to address the problems of growing inequality and of low pay that lie behind the poverty of those at the bottom of the labour market and the social divisions between poor minorities and the more comfortable mass of the population.

Responses to the crises: resolving the welfare state trilemma

Chapter 3 set out the welfare state trilemma: policies must be generous and inclusive, because that is the point of humane state welfare. They must be feasible, in the sense that sufficient political support can be mobilised to put them into practice, otherwise they are irrelevant. They must also be effective in meeting the double crisis outlined above and must do so in a humane and generous way, otherwise there is no point. These constraints form a trilemma because there are real problems in gaining support for tax-financed spending for redistributive services that many voters believe will transfer to groups who don't really deserve them. Feasibility contradicts inclusiveness and generosity.

Second, from a pro-welfare standpoint, effectiveness requires generous and inclusive policies that meet needs collectively and lead public opinion to support yet more humane and inclusive reform. Existing divisions by class, gender, ethnicity and region in access to and outcomes from the use of the more universal aspects of welfare state provision contradict inclusiveness. Addressing these divisions may damage support from the groups who fear they will lose out.

Third, generous and inclusive services require more resources to be effective, whether or not progress is made in mitigating income inequalities in the market and in regulating the universal services to achieve more equal outcomes. Extra taxes are necessary, but may damage political feasibility. Current policies, which deepen divisions, intensify stigma and fragment collective provision, make the trilemma yet more intransigent.

DOI: 10.1057/9781137328113

The immediate public spending crisis

Chapters 3 and 4 reviewed a number of proposals designed to address these issues. The immediate crisis focuses attention on welfare for the poor who face mounting needs and benefit cuts and attract meagre public sympathy. New proposals seek to reframe the issue through a number of interconnected reforms: highlighting child poverty, since children are not seen as responsible for their own circumstances; linking welfare to contribution where possible to demonstrate that those at the bottom also play a reciprocal role in society; re-emphasising that most of those below the poverty line live in working households and are not simply dependants on the tax-payer; and strengthening the connection between benefits and the needs of children and families or work and training opportunities. The object is to highlight the fact that most low-income people share aspirations for secure family life with the mass of the population, are committed to paid work and take responsibility for their own needs.

These approaches confront stigma and social division by stressing the commonality of need, life-style and values between the poor and the mass of the population in order to make generous, inclusive and effective provision feasible. There are indications that some direct redistribution to address child poverty might be politically acceptable and affordable. However, eliminating working-age poverty simply by increasing benefits would require extra resources on a scale that is not feasible without structural reforms to reduce inequality in wages and expand opportunities for members of low-income households, especially women with care responsibilities, to earn more.

Further proposals address this issue and take the debate outside the traditional area of redistribution. They include: social investment to achieve a real return for government and the economy in areas like childcare, social care and education; preventive strategies that might cut future commitments by changing health behaviour, reducing repeat offending or enabling people to manage the need for child or elder care more efficiently; and pre-distributive programmes to raise earnings at the bottom end (notably a higher minimum wage and stronger trade union rights), improve working conditions and perhaps regulate utility prices and rents. The objective is to make policies which help the poor more feasible, by including a wider range of social groups and by limiting the scale of inequality in the first place.

DOI: 10.1057/9781137328113

All these proposals offer humane and generous ways forward for welfare. They focus on different areas of social need. Contribution-centred approaches are most viable for those close to paid work or heavily engaged in care-work. Child-centred policies apply to families of working age and training-centred policies to those entering or at transitions in working life. The social investment logic is most compelling in relation to childcare, education and lifelong learning, preventative policies in some areas of health care and pre-distribution in helping those in low-paid jobs. The new approaches share the fact that they reframe the issues to stress common identities and aspirations between low-income and more comfortable people rather than pointing specifically at redistribution to the poor. Contributory welfare follows a standard life-course, family and work are normal aspirations, childcare or training as social investments generate a return and provide services that many people need to follow those aspirations, and prevention and pre-distribution can be directed to needs that affect many people. However these policies will always miss some of the most vulnerable groups. Directly redistributive welfare will also be needed to move towards greater equality.

The new policies require additional resources, and the sums involved depend greatly on the level of unemployment and of wages. The estimates discussed in Chapter 3 indicate that ending child poverty as it currently stands would cost about £10bn or 0.7 per cent of GDP. A benefit programme that understood inclusion in terms of raising the incomes of all working-age adults above the current poverty line through redistributive state benefits, however organised, would increase potential expenditure by perhaps £28bn or some 2 per cent of GDP. Some of the proposals also require the effective regulation of minimum wage levels, pricing strategies and rents. Regulatory welfare is cheaper than direct provision, but not costless.

Spending commitments at these levels are not feasible in the immediate future. Further progress would require a new approach to political economy that sets a longer term for reducing the deficit and accepts a larger role for state spending. An immediate programme designed to address the needs of low-income people highlighted by the public spending crisis might focus primarily on eliminating child poverty by 2020 as envisaged in the 2010 Child Poverty Act, on strengthening the contributory aspects of the current benefit system to reverse the shift to means-testing, and on preventative, pre-distributive and social investment measures. This would address humane goals in a way that engages public sympathy and meet the over-riding need to help shift public discourse towards, rather than away from, inclusive and collective provision.

The longer-term crisis

The issues that those committed to the future expansion of state welfare face in relation to the longer-term crisis are rather different. The expansion of public spending to meet future needs in health care, education and pensions involves larger sums than are required to move towards more inclusive provision for low-income groups, but is judged feasible because the services are already highly valued. Current reforms will fragment the services, give commercial providers a much larger role and may well make the problems of cost-efficiency more difficult. The object for defenders of more generous and humane welfare is to retain collective provision, expand it where it is currently limited, as in child and social care, and promote greater equality and inclusiveness so that the social divisions in access to and outcomes from universal services diminish. While these policies will be seen primarily in terms of their effect in strengthening already popular universal services, they also improve opportunities and incomes for those at the bottom.

The discussion in Chapter 4 leads in four main directions. The first examines some of the experiences of targeted or inclusive universalism in recent social policy. It shows that a combination of extra spending on the major services plus specific targeted initiatives to raise standards for the less favoured groups had some success during the early 2000s, particularly in schooling. Vigorous pursuit of a similar strategy may go some way in addressing the issues of inequality of outcome in health and education highlighted earlier. Since targeting can be directed to include groups by area (as in action zone and neighbourhood policies) as well as by income (as in childcare tax credit, education maintenance allowance or capitation premia to GPs and local government for deprived service users) these policies can also help address the widening spatial social divisions discussed in Chapter 2.

The second main policy direction concerns the use of state regulatory powers to curb some of the advantages of privileged groups, through access to the most advantageous areas of state provision and the use of private schools, clinics or medical insurance funded as charities, and to control costs and quality more effectively when the state contracts with the private sector, as in the current outsourcing programmes, the purchase

DOI: 10.1057/9781137328113

of drugs and managing PPP schemes. Experience indicates that effective regulation of powerful private actors is difficult and that the problems are particularly intractable in relation to the more complex areas of state provision which current policies address. Competition on price prioritises savings over quality. The current model of extensive outsourcing is unlikely to deliver good quality and inclusive services cost-effectively.

The third point is that pressure to contain escalating costs in the human services will continue over time. In this sense Pierson's influential portrayal of the future of the welfare state as 'permanent austerity' is correct (2001, 456), but this does not preclude progress towards greater social inclusion and the management of demographic and other pressures. A variety of methods have been employed to contain the rate at which costs increase, including internal markets and managerial reforms, annual efficiency savings, use of targets, outsourcing, the introduction of new technologies and now social bonds and payment by results. All these methods can contribute. The first three have been most widely applied. Competitive internal markets with fixed prices in areas like health care and education appear to achieve cost-efficiencies but require regulation and constant monitoring to maintain standards and ensure that the most sought-after providers do not direct their efforts to the least challenging users. Efficiency savings need to be monitored so that providers maintain standards and do not focus on the more readily achieved short-term cuts. Targets also risk distorting activity so that outcomes are damaged.

These policies will also require extra spending and a strengthening of regulatory powers. The sums involved are likely to be small compared to those needed to meet the long-run trend to cost escalation in human services. They will require serious commitment by the government and the political leadership necessary to achieve sufficient consensus to ensure that policies are pursued over time in the face of opposition from the interests affected. This leads to the fourth point.

Policies to develop a more positive response to the crisis require major reforms and substantial additional public spending, some of it in areas that are currently unpopular. Mitigation of poverty requires maximally some 2.5 per cent of GDP and minimally 0.7 per cent to tackle child poverty, with some extra resources to develop longer-term regulatory and targeted inclusive policies. Managing cost escalation in mass services requires 0.4 per cent of GDP each decade. Targeted universalism and effective implementation will add to the cost, but investment and pre-distributive policies would eventually reduce it somewhat.

DOI: 10.1057/9781137328113

Substantial progress towards more humane state welfare could be made by rejecting the current policy of cutting public spending in the UK below that of all other major capitalist countries and instead maintaining it at the level it has traditionally enjoyed for most of the post-war period: at the mid-point of the G7 range, slightly below Germany and substantially below France and the EU average, but above the US, Canada and Japan (Figure 1.2). Instead of sinking below 40 per cent of GDP on a par with the US by about 2015–16, as current policy envisages, it would remain some 3 per cent higher. This would require a decision to reduce the rate at which the deficit is paid off, the abandonment of any future programme of tax reductions and a commitment to raise the necessary revenue through staged and progressive tax increases. Further progress would depend on the restoration of stable growth and continued public support, in short widespread recognition that public spending makes an essential contribution to a humane society and is not simply a burden on the national enterprise. Spending at this level would make it possible to meet the long-term pressures, and address child poverty as outlined above, pursue the social investment, prevention and pre-distribution reforms, inject some resources into establishing an extended contributory welfare benefit system and pursue the regulation of privilege and targeted programmes to promote more inclusive universalism in the mass services as discussed in Chapter 4.

Such a programme would be pursued over time and through policies that fostered rather than undermined the development of more inclusive sympathies across the population. In the short term nearly 1 per cent of GDP could be raised by halving the tax reliefs for occupational and private pension contributions and funds. This would be sufficient to make substantial inroads into child poverty and to pursue regulatory reforms and effective restructuring. The fact that people have been willing to pay more for the expansion of the popular mass services in the past indicates that it should be possible to levy gradual tax increases to maintain standards in these areas in response to the longer-term crisis, assuming that real wages are also rising.

Improvements in efficiency in tax gathering and the more stringent regulation of avoidance might generate extra revenue. HMRC estimates that the sum in question amounts to about £32bn (equivalent to nearly 2 per cent of GDP: HCPAC 2012c, Summary). However it is unclear how much new money could be gained in this way since much of the tax foregone is an assumed liability of multi-national companies and of the

DOI: 10.1057/9781137328113

very wealthy, who are influential, mobile and often successful in litigation. This suggests that the move to the G7 mid-point in spending to support a generous and inclusive programme across the board is feasible as a long-term aspiration but one that would require willingness on the part of the mass of the population to pay higher taxes to fund more redistributive services. This raises the question of how political support for the new policies might be secured.

Identifying a driving force to make change possible: new risks and new policies

The discussion at the beginning of Chapter 3 pointed out that a new direction in policy requires three things: circumstances which provide the opportunity to promote reform; a policy logic to frame the desired approach as an effective response to current challenges; and mobilised voters and interests who will drive through the change. The current combination of cutbacks plus restructuring seizes the opportunity of the current crisis, builds on a radical liberal policy logic in which cutting the deficit trumps any reflationary initiatives and draws support from the middle mass, whose welfare state is relatively protected and who have little sympathy for the poor, and from commercial and business interests, who benefit from privatisation and from downward pressure on wages. The object, from this perspective, is to shift the UK towards a radical liberalism that reflects US rather than European approaches to public policy.

The discussion in Chapter 2 emphasised the growing importance of inequality and social division and showed how these may influence the climate of ideas, gearing up the existing resentment of the middle mass against low-income minorities. Alternatively, policies which add cuts in benefits and social provision to the decline in real wages for many people may also marshal new political groupings in defence of more generous and inclusive welfare. Approaches which stress contribution and social investment and combine targeting with universal provision seek to reframe popular perceptions of redistributive state welfare. Longer-term social change may also help mobilise those who support more humane welfare state policies across a broader range of social groupings.

From this perspective, the deepening of social divisions is only part of the story. Other changes during the past half-century lead more people to experience shared needs for social provision of rather different kinds

DOI: 10.1057/9781137328113

during the course of their lives. This affects welfare politics, since it indicates potential sources of support for more inclusive policies. Immediately after the Second World War manufacturing industry providing relatively secure employment which paid a family wage to the predominantly male workforce was at the heart of the economy and of social and political divisions. Britain was an industrial nation, social class was the strongest influence on voting and the labour market was characterised by deep gender divisions. Now most people are employed in the service sector, many more women are in paid work, although equal pay and opportunities have not yet been achieved, and wage inequalities between higher and lower-skilled work are much greater, as discussed in Chapter 2.

Social risk theories examine how these changes emerge in people's lives and influence how people understand the needs they face, the context in which government seeks to manage those demands and the politics of welfare (Bonoli 2005, 2007, Esping-Andersen 1999, chapter 8, Taylor-Gooby 2004, chapter 1). Traditional trade union politics in the 1950s and 1960s emphasised horizontal distribution, since workplace struggles for adequate wages secured the needs of most families during the working life-stage. Demands for state intervention centred on old social risks: health services, a standard education and pensions to meet needs in old age and perhaps disability, sickness and transitional unemployment. The male bread-winner family form with its gendered division between production (waged) and consumption-oriented (unwaged) labour stressed the same pattern of needs. The welfare settlement undervalued provision for social and childcare, since these needs were served largely by the unpaid family labour of women. Consequently, the traditional form of the welfare state centred primarily on the needs of male workers (O'Connor *et al.* 1999, 19–23).

The risks faced in a normal life course have grown more complex, making fresh demands on the welfare state. The emerging politics of 'new social risks' addresses a new range of needs which confront people in post-industrial society and which families are unable to supply for themselves. These pressures affect people much earlier in the life course than do the health, social care and pension risks at the centre of traditional welfare state politics, and have a direct impact on women as mothers and workers. They foster demand for:

▸ The services and rights that are needed to help those, mainly
    women, engaged in care fulfil a full role in employment and in
    society: good quality child and elder care; equality and anti-

DOI: 10.1057/9781137328113

discrimination policies; a family friendly workplace and good parental rights.

▸ The benefits, services and rights that help people access opportunities in an increasingly competitive society, where job quality depends increasingly on skill and inequalities are fanning out: education, training and lifelong learning available to all, support in finding and keeping a job and progressing in it, greater equality of opportunity.

▸ The benefits and rights that those on low pay in a more divided labour market and marginal and sub-employed workers need: tax credit, housing benefits, job seekers' allowance, sick and disabled benefits, a living wage and good employment protection; policies to curb inequalities and give employees more influence in the workplace: stronger trade unions, works councils and better employment protection.

These needs have emerged in recent years alongside the old social risks which were the backbone of the traditional welfare state. They could form the basis for new coalitions of interest to advance more inclusive social provision. The experience of the past two decades is that new and potentially more generous policies have been developed to meet needs in the first two areas but not in the third: the gendered areas of better child-care and family-friendly working rights, and an expansion of education and training, increasingly directed to help young people get access to decent jobs, but much less enthusiasm for policies to help those who are unsuccessful in an intensely competitive labour market.

The politics of new social risks also applies to governments who face new pressures that may generate support for social interventions as well as for radical liberalism. Successful engagement in highly competitive international markets is crucial to almost all national economies. This has powerful effects on the room for manoeuvre of government in relation to employment and industrial structure. Attempts to influence wages or maintain particular industries against external competitive pressures are likely to encounter penalties in currency devaluation, high interest rates, weak foreign investment and the diminished viability of domestic industries. The outcome (and here Britain has moved more rapidly than many European countries) is a bias towards liberalism in economic policy, but at the same time to the social policies outlined above. One reason for the commitment to childcare and education but not to redistribution for those on low incomes that we identified in

DOI: 10.1057/9781137328113

recent policies is that the first two areas relate directly to the size and quality of the workforce and gain support from governments committed to growth and business interests. Redistribution on the other hand is seen to damage competitiveness.

The emergence of new social risks and attendant provision reshapes welfare state politics. New social risks impact families at an earlier life-stage. In addition to the needs that most people have always expected to encounter, mainly in old age, for pensions and health and social care, new pressures impact individuals with varying severity depending on the state of the economy, skill level, the dependency of family members and family resources. As the stable working class/middle-class coalitions that had supported the development of the established old social risk welfare state tended to break up, political parties across Europe needed to construct balanced programmes of reform designed to appeal across the electorate. In short, new social risks become more influential alongside old social risks in the politics of welfare as part of a more complex pattern of interests placing greater demands on political leadership to build coalitions of support for public spending.

Growing inequalities, greater divisions between the poor and the mass of the population, shifts in the pattern of social risks and unease about the economic direction of the UK set the scene for new directions in policy. The government's programme of cutback and restructuring involves considerable political risks, not least in holding a coalition government together and in managing the pain of deteriorations in public services. The social and economic context helps to explain what current policies aim to achieve and how they have developed. Greater inequality heightens conflicts round social policy and strengthens support for a shift towards market liberalism on the part of the winners. However, it also creates the opportunity to identify common interests among the losers and to push forward new, more interventionist policies. The growing importance of new social risks strengthens the opportunity to recognise shared needs. The UK is at the forefront of both liberalism and the growth of new social risks since its economy has moved most rapidly from manufacturing to more diverse service sector employment, inequalities have widened from European to US levels and state provision to meet needs for social and childcare, training and lifelong learning and support for those who command low wages is weak.

The shifts in patterns of social risk bear particularly heavily on those with family responsibilities, on the low-skilled and the poor, especially

DOI: 10.1057/9781137328113

so at a time of economic stagnation. They offer opportunities to develop new coalitions of interest between mass and minority needs.

New risks and inclusive politics

A number of commentators argue that greater pressures on the poor and widening social divisions separate the experience of those with weak skills and opportunities from the mass of the population in an increasingly divided labour market, making it much harder to gain support for redistributive welfare (Emmenegger *et al.* 2012). One task for more humane and inclusive policy is to broaden the experience of universal services that effectively meet shared needs. New social risk provision offers a way of achieving this, especially for education and training, access to decent jobs and the highly gendered areas of child and elder care and family-friendly working and their impact on a normal working life.

As we noted in Chapter 3, childcare costs have risen rapidly; pressures from this direction are a common feature of the life-course of normal two-earner families. Demand for elder care is less predictable and more uneven. The fact that governments from different parties have developed policies in both these areas during the past two decades (the bi-partisan lowering of the age for preschooling, the targeted universal Sure Start and childcare tax credit programmes, the pupil premium, the prominence given to support for childcare and elder care in the 2013 Coalition re-launch (Cabinet Office 2013) and the series of reports and commissions on long-term care culminating in the Dilnot Commission, accepted in principle by the current government: Dilnot 2011) testifies to the effectiveness of pressure for better services. Similarly the importance of skill level and opportunity in access to work has led to continuing demands for improvements in these areas (BIS 2012, CBI 2012).

Education is generally seen as a highly popular mass service at the core of state welfare. Significantly, schooling is declared exempt from the 2010 Coalition's cuts, in practice undergoing relatively small cuts in current spending (under 2 per cent) but much larger cutbacks in building and maintenance programmes (60 per cent: Chowdry and Sibieta 2011, 4). Educational programmes can also widen opportunities and direct resources towards less privileged groups. They can include lifelong learning and training/retraining for those whose skills are obsolete in a rapidly changing labour market. Childcare is a widely recognised need, overlapping with education as preschooling expands, and with demands for more family-friendly working conditions as it helps women gain better access to employment. It is also an important element in any programme to address family poverty by enabling parents to participate in paid work.

Education and childcare are both part of the mass welfare state but include elements that bear differentially on life-chances at the bottom, bridging between new and old social risks and the constituencies associated with them. They provide opportunities to develop provision that can be both feasible and inclusive because it meets needs recognised by many people that are also particularly onerous for the poorest groups.

Policies for those marginal to or excluded from access to decently paid work, the third area of new social risk identified above, present a different picture. The emphasis here is on activation through the 1997–2010 government's New Deal or the current privatised Work Programme. Both programmes include elements of training, work readiness and support in paid employment, but both also use the gap between benefits and bottom-end wages supplemented by in-work benefits to sharpen incentives and impose increasingly harsh controls on unemployed claimers. The new risks for this group are not obviously shared by the mass of the population and do not lead immediately towards a more inclusive politics.

The current context

Some new risks cross-cut high-need minorities and the mass of the population. As state welfare is cutback, fragmented and rendered more intensely work-centred, more people are likely to experience real pressures in relation to the cost of childcare and decent housing and access to education that leads to a decent wage during the course of their lives. How far the experience of insecurity will bridge the division between minority and mass interests is at present unclear. Real median incomes are expected to fall by more than 7 per cent between 2009 and 2013 and then recover slowly, a deeper and longer collapse in living standards than at any time since the 1974–7 recession (Joyce 2012, 15). These circumstances present a good opportunity to develop an inclusive programme that is also politically feasible because it centres on the normal aspirations of family life. Such a programme would stress the fact that the 2010–15 cuts bear most heavily on women and families. It would include education, training, childcare and possibly support for low-income families, as

DOI: 10.1057/9781137328113

well as the health care and pensions that have always predominated in social policy.

One indication of the feasibility of such a project lies in the fact that recent patterns of welfare state provision acknowledge the importance of new social risks in relation to children. The proportion of social spending directed to child and family needs, social care and welfare benefits has increased rapidly across welfare regimes in Europe during the past two decades (Nikolai 2011, Taylor-Gooby 2004, table 1.1). Spending on cash benefits in the UK has roughly tripled as a percentage of GDP since the Second World War, growing rapidly in the 1950s, 1960s and 1970s, more slowly during the 1980s and 1990s, and then accelerating in the 2000s until very recently (Browne and Hood 2012, figure 4.2). Partly this resulted from the build up of entitlements to pensions and some other benefits, partly from higher payments as living standards and expectations rose and partly from spending on new benefits directed mainly at the new risks.

The most striking trends in the past three decades have been the growth of spending on children (mainly tax credits and child benefits) and on housing and council tax (Browne and Hood 2012, figure 4.3). Child Tax Credit now accounts for about 11 per cent of total benefit spending (about 1.5 per cent of GDP), child benefit for about 6 per cent and Housing and Council Tax benefits nearly 14 per cent. Despite long-run pressures to prioritise spending on older people and squeeze welfare for the poor, the welfare state has increasingly recognised the needs of low-income families and of children in them, at the same time seeking to mobilise more people into paid work. Estimating the scale of the increase in spending on child poverty is difficult since Child Tax Credit was preceded by a stream of less generous benefits, Family Income Supplement, then Family Credit. In addition Child Tax Credit incorporated the child elements of Working Tax Credit in 2003, Job Seeker's Allowance and Income Support in 2004 and some other benefits (Browne and Hood 2012, 74). The child elements of these benefits (or the equivalent) did not exceed 1 per cent of GDP by 1997/8 (calculated from Browne and Hood 2012, figure 4.3 and table 2.1). Spending on child poverty has risen by at least 0.5 per cent of GDP during the decade before the recession, about two-thirds of the amount required to end child poverty.

The experience of the past three decades is that the everyday life needs of families have moved up the political agenda as the costs of childcare, housing and other services affect more and more people, stretching far

DOI: 10.1057/9781137328113

beyond those who are unemployed. Vertical redistribution to meet the specific needs of poor out-groups edges closer to the horizontal redistribution required to enable most people to manage the demands they face during a normal life-course. As in the case of the mass services, health care, education and pensions, spending the sums needed to make substantial inroads into child poverty is business as usual for the UK welfare state. The challenge is to build on the way the shifts in the patterns of social risks that people experience during their lives blur the distinction between mass and minority needs and between horizontal and vertical redistribution and to devise programmes that lead the public to endorse more generous and inclusive provision across more comfortable and less advantaged groups.

Conclusions

This book examines the double crisis confronting social policy. The precipitate response of the 2010 Government to pressures on public spending instigated the immediate crisis by cutting benefits for the poor and restructuring state provision in a way that fragments services and undermines collectivism. One objective is to move towards a more competitive, individualistic, liberal society in which people's understanding of their social world and of their political interests shifts decisively to the right. The second longer-run crisis chiefly concerns a different range of services and benefits which redistribute mainly over the life cycle and are highly popular but are likely to consume an increasingly proportion of national resources. In both areas the main direction of policy is to preserve spending on mass services at the expense of those for poorer minorities. In the current crisis health care, education and pensions face less stringent cuts. In the longer-term these are the areas where spending appears certain to rise, and where the public may well be willing to accept the extra tax involved but much more reluctant to pay for benefits which redistribute to those on low income. Either way the project of a more inclusive and generous welfare state faces serious challenges.

It may well be that government fails to impose cuts at the level anticipated. The experience of the previous episodes of cutback from the 1920s onwards reviewed in Chapter 2 suggests that public spending in the UK is resilient to change. However, stringent cuts, particularly those in benefits for low-income groups, were already in place by early 2013. The restructuring of public provision so that many people have

DOI: 10.1057/9781137328113

less experience of common structures of provision and see low-income claimers as work-shy dependants may undermine support for collective welfare and set the scene for further cutbacks.

The new liberalism is often seen to work with the grain of social change, an appropriate political economy for a more globally competitive, individualistic, post-industrial, unequal and socially segregated society. However, part of the shift in the climate of ideas during the past three decades concerns the emergence of new social risks which complicate welfare politics because they affect specific groups at particular life stages and do not form the basis for a coherent social movement in the way that class divisions in a manufacturing economy once did. In some areas, most obviously access to good quality affordable child and elder care, education, training and opportunities that lead to secure well-paid jobs and the employment rights and family-friendly support services that enable people to succeed in them, the new pattern of risks cuts across the division between horizontally redistributive mass and vertically redistributive minority welfare.

One indication that this has political impact is the expansion of spending and of provision in these areas during the past three decades under a series of governments. Social change weakens the politics of class division that sustained traditional horizontally redistributive welfare states, but does not simply drive forward a dualised society in which the poor are permanent losers. It also provides the context for a more humane response to the crisis in which the experience of inclusive and generous provision will promote more widespread recognition of the value of collective responses to the common needs almost all of us encounter during the life-course. Support for children and families is the most salient area, pointing to policies to address child poverty, to promote social investment in access to good quality childcare and to improve work opportunities through stronger workplace rights for parents. Such a programme would build on the fact that women are at the forefront of many areas of new social risk and also bear the brunt of the Coalition cuts.

The double crisis of the welfare state confronts advocates of a more humane social programme with tough challenges, exacerbated by growing inequalities and social divisions and by government policies intent on entrenching these divisions within the structure of a second-rate welfare state. More humane and generous alternatives are available, but could only be made effective through a long-term programme to restore UK public spending eventually to a level at the middle of the range of

DOI: 10.1057/9781137328113

G7 countries and through political commitment to pursue directions that may be unpopular with some groups of voters and with powerful private sector interests.

The two wings of the double crisis are often opposed to each other. The mass horizontally redistributive services are popular. The strongest argument for claiming that, with political leadership, it is possible to achieve the necessary spending increases (0.4 per cent of GDP each decade for the foreseeable future) is to point out that spending at this level is simply business as usual. Failing to meet the demand is a political choice in a sense that meeting it is not. A continuation of the trend in spending growth established during times of normal economic expansion in the areas of health and social care, education and pensions will be sufficient to meet the challenges of population ageing and real wage pressures and provide extra to address rising aspirations. A further indication of public willingness to fund provision in these areas is the evidence that, in times of normal growth, people choose to spend increasing amounts on private provision in them in addition to the extra taxes they pay for better state services.

By contrast, poverty among people of working age is heavily stigmatised and most people are reluctant to pay higher taxes to advance social equality. The obvious conclusion is that the welfare state will become increasingly divided and that welfare for the poor will come under greater pressure in the struggle to finance health and social care, pensions and education. This ignores three points: first, poverty is not seamless in public perceptions. Child poverty is less likely to be seen as a matter of personal responsibility and attracts less antipathy. Low-income people who make every effort to contribute to society are less subject to stigma. Second, policies can be developed, with appropriate political leadership, that reframe poverty in terms of social contribution rather than individual failure and present the poor as sharing normal aspirations for family life and jobs that pay enough to support it rather than as work-shy. Third, different directions in policy that raise bottom-end wages towards a living wage and strengthen workplace representation, or emphasise the wider social benefits of reform through social investment or prevention, can help reduce the costs of addressing poverty directly.

Developments during the past three decades in the involvement of women in full-time employment, in the more unequal distribution of wages and in the encroachment of insecurity in paid work shift the pattern of risks that many people experience during the life course. These changes suggest that higher spending to mitigate family poverty

DOI: 10.1057/9781137328113

during working life, expand child and elder care as social investment and address wage levels at the bottom might be acceptable. Again the strongest evidence for the feasibility of such a programme is that spending on policies to address these risks has increased rapidly across Europe. This is reflected in the shift in the balance of spending on benefits towards those of working age and towards support for childcare in social welfare in the UK.

In this sense more positive policies can also work with the grain of people's response to social change, and can bring together the two aspects of crisis: sustaining spending on mass services to meet the long-term pressures and addressing child and family poverty and low wages. The estimates presented in Chapters 3 and 4 indicate that the costs are real but not impossible, given political commitment. They amount to 0.4 per cent each decade for health care, education and pensions, plus some 0.7 per cent of GDP for child poverty. Extra spending of up to 2 per cent of GDP is required to address poverty among those of working age. These costs could be moderated by the impact of a higher minimum wage and of investment in childcare on women's employment, benefit spending and tax receipts. A programme which addressed child poverty and the gradually rising cost of maintaining standards in mass services might be politically feasible. Poverty among those of working age is a long-term issue and requires a shift in attitudes towards those on low incomes and the contribution they make to society.

An inclusive and generous programme would also need further policy initiatives. In health, education and pensions, regulatory policies are required to limit the advantages of better-off people through access to the best state services and tax-subsidised purchase of private provision. This approach has the potential to release substantial sums in extra tax as reliefs are cut back, although the amount raised in practice may be much less than the 1 or 2 per cent of GDP accounted for by the subsidies. It may be sufficient to part-fund targeted spending to provide better health care and schooling for the groups least well served by the current system.

Progress in these areas, and especially in relation to working-age poverty, requires greater public willingness to accept redistribution. This in turn requires a long-term programme to shift public ideas in a more inclusive direction so that higher spending on directly redistributive social welfare and to improve outcomes from health care, education and pension provision for those on low incomes is accepted. Again this requires political leadership to drive home the point that those on high, middle and low

DOI: 10.1057/9781137328113

incomes are all members of society and citizens in a shared welfare state and that all contributions to the social whole are valued.

This book demonstrates that, with careful reflection, problems that appear at first sight as simply intransigent can be presented as virtually insoluble. Policies to address the long-term crisis driven by population ageing and other pressures contradict the spending needed to sustain provision for the poor. Social divisions confront those who wish to advance an inclusive, generous and politically feasible welfare state with a trilemma between solidaristic goals, the means necessary to reach them and realistic tax and spending demands.

Britain achieved the levels of spending necessary to tackle these issues, at the mid-point of the G7 nations, during much of the post-war period. State spending at such levels continues to be considered normal in most Western countries. In key areas of provision we simply need to continue the trends established during the period of growth to resolve the problems that face us and address some of the most pressing issues of child and family poverty. Changes in the patterns of risk that people experience during their life course bolster public support for such policies. The immediate economic crisis only serves to strengthen the pressures. To move further in this direction, confronting the interests entrenched in privileged provision for better-off groups and in the private sector, improving health and educational outcomes for the less advantaged and redistributing towards those on low incomes to mitigate adult working-age poverty, will require political commitment. The difficulties in realising such policies can be moderated through a range of measures: programmes that stress the contribution made to society by low-income workers and carers, social investment and prevention to improve opportunities in work, and higher minimum wages to cut the costs of redistributive spending.

The welfare state trilemma points out that pro-welfare goals (generous and inclusive services) demand means (redistribution, higher tax, confronting established interests) that appear politically unfeasible at first sight, since most people dislike tax and have little sympathy for the poor. The dual crisis of the welfare state is also an opportunity to work towards a resolution of the trilemma. The discussion in this book identifies more humane and feasible policies that can, given the appropriate political leadership, build greater social cohesion and lead towards a more equal and less divided welfare state.

DOI: 10.1057/9781137328113

Bibliography

Acheson, D. (1998) *Inequalities in Health: Report of an Independent Inquiry*, HMSO, London.

Adam, S. (2012) *Personal Taxes and Benefits*, IFS, London, http://www.ifs.org.uk/publications/6488, accessed 16 February 2013.

Adam, S. and Browne, J. (2010) *Redistribution, Work Incentives and Thirty Years of Tax and Benefit Reform*, IFS WP 10/24.

Adonis, A. (2012) *Education, Education, Education*, Biteback, London.

Alakeson, V. and Hurrel, A. (2012) *Counting the Costs of Childcare*, Resolution Foundation, London.

Alvaredo, F., Atkinson, A., Piketty, T. and Saez, E. (2012) *The World Top Incomes Database*, http://g-mond.parisschoolofeconomics.eu/topincomes, accessed 12 August 2012.

Appleby, J. and Alvarez-Rosette, A. (2005) 'Health and Choice', in Park, A., Curtice, J., Thomson, K., Bromley, C., Phillips, M. and Johnson, M. (Eds), *British Social Attitudes No 22*, Sage, London.

Appleby, J., Thompson, J. and Galea, A. *et al.* (2012) *How Is the NHS Performing?* King's Fund, London.

Arulampalam, W., Gregg, P. and Gregory, M. (2001) 'Unemployment Scarring', *The Economic Journal*, 111, F577–84.

Arza, C. and Kohli, M. (2007) *Pension Reform in Europe*, Routledge, London.

Atkinson, A. (2007) 'The Distribution of Earnings in OECD Countries', *International Labour Review*, 146, 2, 41–60.

Atkinson, A. (2008) *The Changing Distribution of Earnings in OECD Countries*, Oxford University Press, Oxford.

Atkinson, A., Piketty, T. and Saez, T. (2011) 'Top Incomes in the Long Run', *Journal of Economic Literature*, 49, 1, 3–71.

Audit Commission (2007) *Healthy Competition*, http://www.audit-commission.gov.uk/sitecollectiondocuments/auditcommissionreports/nationalstudies/healthycompetition2007, accessed 30 December 2012.

Aylett, A. (2010) 'Participatory Planning, Justice and Climate Change in Durban', *Environment and Planning*, A, 42, 99–115.

Bailey, J., Coward, J. and Whittaker, M. (2011) *Painful Separation*, Resolution Foundation, London.

Baiocchi, G. (2001) 'Participation, Activism and Politics', *Politics and Society*, 29, 1, 43–72.

Baird, A., Haynes, J., Massey, F. and Wild, R. (2010) *Public Service Output, Input and Productivity: Education*, ONS, London.

Ball, S. (2008) *The Education Debate*, Policy Press, Bristol.

Bambra, C. (2012) 'Clear Winners and Losers are Created by Age-Only NHS Resource Allocation', *BMJ*, 344, E3593.

Bamfield, J. and Horton, T. (2009) *Understanding Attitudes to Inequality*, JRF, York.

Bartlett, W., Roberts, J. and Le Grand, J. (1998) *A Revolution in Social Policy*, Policy Press, Bristol.

Baumberg, B. (2012) 'Three Ways to Defend Welfare in Britain', *Journal of Poverty and Social Justice*, 20, 2, 149–61.

Baumberg, B., Bell, K. and Gaffney, D. (2012) *Benefits Stigma in Britain*, TurnToUs, London.

BBC (2011) *Independent Schools Win Charity Commission Fight*, 14 October, http://www.bbc.co.uk/news/education-15305699, accessed 30 December 2012.

Béland, D. and Gran, B. (Eds) (2008) *Fragmented Welfare Regimes: The Public-Private Dichotomy in Social Policy*, Palgrave Macmillan, Basingstoke.

Bell, K. and Gaffney, D. (2012) *Making a Contribution*, Touchstone, London.

Ben-Galim, D. (2011) *Making the Case for Universal Childcare*, IPPR, London.

Bevan, G. and Hood, C. (2006) 'Have Targets Improved Performance in the English NHS?' *British Medical Journal*, 332, 419–22.

DOI: 10.1057/9781137328113

BIS (2012) *Skills for Sustainable Growth*, BIS, London.

Black, D. (1980) *Inequalities in Health: Report of a Research Working Group*, DHSS, London.

Blanden, J. and Machin, S. (2007) *Recent Changes in Intergenerational Mobility in Britain*, Sutton Trust Report.

Blanden, J., Buscha, F., Sturgis, P. and Urwin, P. (2012) 'Measuring the Earnings Returns to Lifelong Learning in the UK', *Economics of Education Review*, 31, 4, 501–14.

Bolton, P. (2011) *Education Maintenance Allowance Statistics*, SNGS 5778, HoC Library, House of Commons, London.

Bonoli, G. (2005) 'The Politics of the New Social Policies. Providing Coverage Against New Social Risks in Mature Welfare States', *Policy and Politics*, 33, 3.

Bonoli, G. (2007) 'Time Matters: Postindustrialisation, New Social Risks and Welfare State Adaptation in Advanced Industrial Democracies' *Comparative Political Studies*, 40, 495–520.

Brewer, M., Browne, J. and Joyce, R. (2011) *Child and Working Age Poverty from 2010 to 2020*, IFS Commentary C121, IFS, London.

Browne, J. (2010) *Distributional Analysis of Tax and Benefit Changes*, IFS, Publication 5313, IFS, London.

Browne, J. and Hood, A. (2012) *A Survey of the UK Benefit System*, BN 13, IFS, London (Updated).

Burgess, S., Propper, C. and Wilson, D. (2006) 'Extending Choice in the English Health Care System', *Journal of Social Policy*, 35, 4, 537–57.

Cabinet Office (2011) *Open Public Services*, Cm. 8145, HMSO, London.

Cabinet Office (2013) *Together in the National Interest*, HMSO, London.

Cameron, D. (2009) 'The Big Society', *Hugo Young Lecture*, http://www.conservatives.com/news/speeches/2009/11/david_cameron_the_big_society.aspx, accessed 28 September 2011.

Cameron, D. (2011) 'How We Will Release the Grip of State Control', *Daily Telegraph*, 20 February.

Childs, D. (2001) *Britain since 1939*, second edition, Palgrave Macmillan, Basingstoke.

Chowdry, H. and Sibieta, L. (2011) *Trends in Education and Schools Spending*, BN121, IFS, London.

Clarke, E. and Gardner, O. (2011) *The Red Book*, http://www.scribd.com/doc/73605264/labour-left-the-red-book-23-november-2011, accessed 30 December 2012.

DOI: 10.1057/9781137328113

Coats, D., Johnson, N. and Hackett, P. (2012) *From the Poor Law to Welfare to Work*, Smith Institute, London.

Compass (2011) *Plan B*, http://www.compassonline.org.uk/news/item.asp?n=13946, accessed 30 December 2012.

CBI (2012) *First Steps: Report of the Ambition for Schools Project*, CBI, London.

Cook, F. (1979) *Who Should Be Helped?* Sage, Beverly Hills, CA.

Cooke, G. (2011) *National Salary Insurance: Briefing Paper*, IPPR, London.

Coughlin, R. (1980) *Ideology, Public Opinion and Welfare Policy*, Institute of International Studies, RS No 42, University of California, Berkeley, CA.

CQC (2012) *The State of Health Care and Adult Social Care in England in 2011/12*, HC763, HMSO London.

Crawford, C., Johnson, P., Machin, S. and Vignoles, A. (2011) *Social Mobility: A Literature Review*, BIS, London.

Crawford, R. (2010) *Where Did the Axe Fall?* IFS, London, http://www.ifs.org.uk/publications/5311, accessed 28 May 2011.

Crawford, R. and Emmerson, C. (2012) *NHS and Social Care Funding 2010–11 to 2021–2*, IFS, London.

Crouch, C. (2011) *The Strange Non-Death of Liberalism*, Polity, Cambridge.

Crowe, T. (2000) *Crime Prevention through Environmental Design*, National Crime Prevention Institute, University of Louisville.

Curtice, J. K. and Heath, O. (2009) 'Do People Want Choice and Diversity of Provision in Public Services?', in Park, A., Curtice, J., Thomson, K., Phillips, M. and Clery, E. (Eds), *British Social Attitudes 25th Report*, Sage, London, 55–78.

Davies, H. (2011) *The Financial Crisis: Who's to Blame?* Polity Press, Cambridge.

Daycare Trust (2012) *Annual Childcare Costs Survey 2012*, Daycare Trust, London.

DCLG (2010) *Dwelling Stock Estimates*, DCLG, London.

DCLG (2012) *Statutory Homelessness Statistics, Third Quarter*, http://www.communities.gov.uk/documents/statistics/pdf/22109391.pdf, accessed 30 December 2012.

DCSF (2007b) *National Evaluation of Excellence in Cities: 2002–2006*, NFER, London.

DH (2009) *Mortality Target Monitoring (Infant Mortality, Inequalities) Update to Include Data for 2008*, DH, London.

Dickson, M. and Smith, S. (2011) *What Determines the Return to Education?* CMPO Paper 11/256, Centre for Market and Public Organisation, Bristol.

Dilnot, A. (2011) *Fairer Care Funding: Report of the Commission on Funding Care and Support*, DH, London.

Dolphin, T. (2011) *10 Ways to Promote Growth*, IPPR, London.

Donnison (1970) *The Public Schools Commission: Second Report*, HMSO, London.

Dorling, D. and Ballas, D. (2008) 'Spatial Divisions of Poverty and Wealth', in Ridge, T. and Wright, S. (Eds), *Understanding Poverty, Wealth and Inequality: Policies and Prospects*, Policy Press, Bristol.

Dunsire, A. and Hood, C. (1989) *Cutback Management in Public Bureaucracies*, Cambridge University Press, Cambridge.

Durkheim, E. (1984, orig. 1933) *The Division of Labour in Society*, Free Press, New York.

DWP (2010) *Universal Credit: Welfare That Works*, Cm. 7957, HMSO, London.

DWP (2011b) *The Work Programme*, DWP, London.

DWP (2011a) *Equality Assessment: Welfare Reform Bill*, DWP, London.

DWP (2012a) *Disability Living Allowance Reform: Impact Assessment*, http://www.dwp.gov.uk/docs/dla-reform-wr2011-ia.pdf, accessed 30 December 2012.

DWP (2012b) *Policy: Child Poverty*, DWP Website, http://www.dwp.gov.uk/policy/child-poverty/, accessed 30 December 2012.

DWP (2012c) *Households below Average Income 1994–5 to 2010–11*, DWP, London.

DWP (2012e) *Work Programme Statistics November 2012*, DWP, London.

DWP (2012f) *Statement on A4E Fraud Allegations*, DWP Newsroom, 9 March.

DWP (2012g) *Employment Support Allowance: Impact Assessment*, http://www.dwp.gov.uk/docs/wca-ia-eia.pdf, accessed 30 December 2012.

DWP (2012h) *Government Launches Consultation for Better Measurement of Child Poverty*, http://www.dwp.gov.uk/newsroom/press-releases/2012/nov-2012/dwp121–12.shtml, accessed 15 February 2013.

DWP (2013) *The Single-Tier Pension*, Cm. 8528, HMSO, London.

EC (2006) *The Impact of Ageing on Public Expenditure*, Special Report 1/2006, Ecofin, Brussels.

EC (2012) *The European Ageing Report*, Ecofin, Brussels.

DOI: 10.1057/9781137328113

Emmenegger, P., Häusermann, S., Palier, B. and Seeleib-Kaiser, M. (2012) *The Age of Dualization: The Changing Face of Inequality in Deindustrializing Societies*, Oxford University Press, Oxford.

Esping-Andersen, G. (1999) *Social Foundations of Postindustrial Economies*, Oxford University Press, Oxford.

Esping-Andersen, G. (2002) *Why We Need a New Welfare State*, Oxford University Press, Oxford.

EU (2000) *Lisbon European Council, Presidency Conclusion 23 March*, http://www.consilium.europa.eu/uedocs/cms_data/docs/pressdata/en/ec/00100-r1.eno.htm, accessed 30 December 2012.

Fabian Society (2000) *Commission on Taxation and Spending*, Fabian Society, London.

Farnsworth, K. (2011) 'From Economic Crisis to a New Age of Austerity: The UK', in Farnsworth, K. and Irving, Z. (Eds), *Social Policy in Challenging Times*, Policy Press, Bristol.

Fawcett Society (2012) *Fawcett's Response to the Autumn Statement, 2012*, Fawcett Society, London.

Fenge, R. and Werding, M. (2004) 'Ageing and the Tax Implied in Public Pension Schemes', *Fiscal Studies*, 25, 2, 159–200.

Fishkin, J. (2009) *When the People Speak*, Oxford University Press, Oxford.

Fiske, E. and Ladd, H. (2000) *When Schools Compete: A Cautionary Tale*, Brookings Institute Press, Washington D.C.

Fitzpatrick, S., Johnsen, S. and White, M. (2011) 'Multiple Exclusion Homelessness in the UK: Key Patterns and Intersections', *Social Policy and Society*, 10, 4, 501–12.

Flynn, N. (2007) *Public Sector Management*, Fifth Edition, Sage, London.

G4S (2012) *Review of London Olympic and Paralympic Games Security Contract*, G4S, London.

Gamble, A. (2011) *Economic Futures?* British Academy, London.

Gardiner, K. and Evans, M. (2011) *Exploring Poverty Gaps among Children in the UK*, WP 103, DWP, London.

Gaynor, M. and Town, R. (2012) *Competition in Health Care Markets*, WP 12/282, CMPO, Bristol.

Gaynor, M., Morena-Serra, R. and Propper, C. (2010) *Death by Market Power*, WP 10/242, CMPO, Bristol.

Gewirtz, S., Ball, S. and Bowe, R. (1995) *Markets, Equality and Choice in Education*, Open University Press, Buckingham.

DOI: 10.1057/9781137328113

Gibbons, S., Machin, S. and Silva, O. (2006) 'The Educational Impact of Parental Choice and School Competition', *Centrepiece*, 11, 3, 6–9, LSE, London.

Giddens, A. (1995) *Beyond Left and Right*, Polity Press, Cambridge.

Giddens, A. (1998) *The Third Way: The Renewal of Social Democracy*, Polity Press, Cambridge.

Gintis, H., Bowles, S., Boyd, R. and Fehr, E. (2005) *Moral Sentiments and Material Interests*, MIT Press, Cambridge, MA.

Glasby, J. and Littlechild, R. (2009) *Direct Payments and Personal Budgets: Putting Personalisation into Practice*, Policy Press, Bristol.

Glasgow Media Group (2010) *Proposal for a Wealth Tax*, GMG, http://www.glasgowmediagroup.org/, accessed 30 December 2012.

Glendinning, C., Arksey, H., Jones, K., Moran, N., Netten, A. and Rabiee, P. (2009) *Individual Budgets Pilot Projects*, Social Policy Research Unit, University of York, York.

Glennerster, H. (2010) *Financing the United Kingdom's Welfare States*, 2020 Public Services Trust, London.

Glynn, A. (2006) *Capitalism Unleashed*, Oxford University Press, Oxford.

Goldacre, B. (2012) *Bad Pharma*, Harper Collins, New York.

Goode, J., Callender, C. and Lister, R. (1998) *Purse or Wallet? Gender Inequalities and the Income Distribution within Families on Benefit*, Policy Studies Institute, London.

Gough, I. (2011a) 'Welfare Cuts', in Farnsworth, K. and Irving, Z. (Eds), *Social Policy in Challenging Times*, Policy Press, Bristol.

Gough, I. (2011b) *Climate Change and Public Policy*, British Academy, London.

Gough, I. (2012) *The Wisdom of Prevention: Theoretical Background*, NEF, London.

Green, F. (2006) *Demanding Work. The Paradox of Job Quality in the Affluent Economy*, Princeton University Press, Princeton.

Green, F. (2013) *Skills and Skilled Work*, Princeton University Press, Princeton.

Grice, J. (2012) *The Productivity Conundrum*, ONS, London.

Hacker, J. (2011) *The Institutional Foundations of Middle Class Democracy*, Policy Network, London.

Hacker, J. and Pierson, P. (2010) *Winner Takes All Politics*, Simon and Schuster, New York.

Harbers, I. (2007) 'Democratic Deepening in Third Wave Democracies', *Political Studies*, 55, 38–58.

DOI: 10.1057/9781137328113

Hardie, M., Cheers, J., Pinder, C. and Qaeser, U. (2011) *Public Sector Outputs, Inputs and Productivity: Healthcare No 5*, ONS, London.

Hassenteufel, P. and Palier, B. (2007) 'Towards Neo-Bismarckian Health Care States?' *Social Policy and Administration*, 41, 6, 574–96.

Hay, C. and Wincott, D. (2012) *European Welfare Capitalism in Hard Times*, Palgrave Macmillan, Basingstoke.

HC Health Committee (2010) *2nd Report 2010–1, Public Expenditure*, HC 512, HMSO, London.

HC Health Committee (2012) *13th Report 2012–13, Public Expenditure: Summary and Conclusions*, HC 1499, HMSO, London.

HCPAC (2011a) *26th Report, 2011–12, Management of NHS Hospital Productivity*, HC 741, HMSO, London.

HCPAC (2011b) *57th Report 2011–12, Oversight of User Choice and Provider Competition in Care Markets*, HC 1530, HMSO, London.

HCPAC (2012a) *15th Report, 2011–12, Preventing Fraud in Contracted Employment Programmes*, HC 103, HMSO, London.

HCPAC (2012b) *16th Report 2011–12, Department of Health: Securing the Future Financial Sustainability of the NHS*, HC 389, HMSO, London.

HCPAC (2012c) *19th Report 2011–12, HM Revenue and Customs: Accounts and Evidence*, HC 38, HMSO, London.

HCPASC (2011) *17th Report 2011–12, The Big Society*, HC 902-I, HMSO, London.

Hedges, A. and Bromley, C. (2001) *Public Attitudes towards Taxation*, Fabian Society, London.

Hills, J. (2011) 'The Changing Architecture of the Welfare State', *Oxford Review of Economic Policy*, 27, 4, 589–607.

Hills, J., Sefton, T. and Stewart, K. (2009) *Towards a More Equal Society?* Policy Press, Bristol.

Hinrichs, K. and Lynch, J. (2010) 'Old-Age Pensions', in Castles, F. *et al.* (Eds), *Oxford Handbook of the Welfare State*, Oxford University Press, Oxford.

Hirsch, D. (2009) *Ending Child Poverty in a Changing Economy*, JRF, York.

HM Treasury (1979) *The Government's Expenditure Plans 1979–80 to 1980–81*,

HM Treasury (2002) *Budget Report 2002*, HMSO, London.

HM Treasury (2010) *Budget 2010*, HC 451, HMSO, London.

HM Treasury (2010) *Spending Review*, Cm. 7942, HMSO, London.

HM Treasury (2012a) *Autumn Statement: Impact on Households*, HMSO, London.

DOI: 10.1057/9781137328113

HM Treasury (2012b) *Autumn Statement*, Cm. 8480, HMSO, London.

HMRC (2012) *Registered Pension Schemes: Cost of Tax Relief*, http://www.hmrc.gov.uk/stats/pensions/pen6.pdf, accessed 30 December 2012.

HoC Library (2011) *The Local Government Finance Settlement 2011–13*, RP 11/16, House of Commons, London.

HoC Library (2012) *Homelessness in England*, SN/SP/1164, House of Commons, London.

Hoggett, P., Beedell, P., Jiminez, J., Mayo, M. and Miller, C. (2006) 'Identity, Life History and Commitment to Welfare', *Journal of Social Policy*, 35, 4, 689–704.

Home Office (2010) *The Drug Strategy*, http://www.homeoffice.gov.uk/publications/alcohol-drugs/drugs/drug-strategy/drug-strategy-2010?view=binary, accessed 30 December 2012.

Hood, C., Emerson, C. and Dixon, R. (2010) *Public Spending in Hard Times*, ESRC Public Services Programme, University of Oxford, Oxford.

Horton, T. and Gregory, J. (2009) *The Solidarity Society*, Fabian Society, London.

IFS (2011) *Green Budget 2011*, IFS, London.

IFS (2012a) *Benefit Integration in the UK*, http://www.esri.ie/docs/budgetconf2012sept_brewer.pdf, accessed 30 December 2012.

IFS (2012b) *Green Budget 2012*, IFS, London.

IMF (2012) *International Monetary Fund World Economic Outlook Database, October 2012*, IMF, Washington.

Independent Commission on Fees (2012) *Analysis of UCAS Applications for 2012/13 Admissions*, Sutton Trust, London.

IPPR (2012) *Paying a Living Wage Could Save the UK Billions*, IPPR, London.

Ipsos-Mori (2010) *Exit Poll*, http://www.ipsos-mori.com/, accessed 30 December 2012.

Ipsos-Mori (2011) *Welfare Reform*, http://www.ipsos-mori.com/researchpublications/researcharchive/2876/Future-State-of-Welfare.aspx, accessed 16 February 2013.

Ipsos-Mori (2012) *Almanac 2012*, Ipsos-Mori, London.

Jaeger, M. (2007) 'Are the Deserving Needy Really Deserving Everywhere?' in Mau, S. and Veghte, B. (Eds), *Social Justice, Legitimacy and the Welfare State*, Ashgate, Aldershot.

Johnstone, R. (2011) 'Council Outsourcing Plans Could Take Decade', *Public Finance*, 11 May.

DOI: 10.1057/9781137328113

Joyce, R. (2012) *Tax and Benefit Reforms Due in 2012–13, and the Outlook for Household Incomes*, BN126, IFS, London.

Julius, D. (2008) *Understanding the Public Services Industry*, BIS, London.

Jurd, A. (2011) *Public Service Labour Productivity*, ONS, London

King's Fund (2011) *Did Labour's Spearhead Health Inequalities Policy Miss the Target but Hit the Point?* http://www.kingsfund.org.uk/blog/2011/07/did-labours-spearhead-health-inequalities-policy-miss-target, accessed 10 January 2013.

King's Fund (2012) *The BSA Survey 2011: Why Has Satisfaction Fallen between 2010 and 2011?* King's Fund, London.

Knapp, M. *et al.* (2010) *Building Community Capacity: Making an Economic Case*, DP 2772, PSSRU, LSE, London.

Laws, D. and Marshall, P. (2004) *The Orange Book: Reclaiming Liberalism*, Profile Books, London.

Le Grand, J. (1982) *The Strategy of Equality: Redistribution and the Social Services*, Allen & Unwin, London.

Le Grand, J. (2003) *Motivation, Agency and Public Policy*, Oxford University Press, Oxford.

Le Grand, J. (2007) *The Other Invisible Hand*, Princeton University Press, Princeton.

Leech, D. and Campos, E. (2003) 'Is Comprehensive Education Really Free?' *Journal of the Royal Statistical Society*, 166, 1, 135–54.

Leitch (2006) *Prosperity for All in the Globalised Economy*, HM Treasury, HMSO, London.

Local Government Association (LGA) (2011) *Funding Settlement Disappointing*, http://www.lga.gov.uk/lga/core/page.do?pageid=16647103, accessed 28 May 2011.

Lupton, R., Heath, N. and Salter, E. (2009) 'Education: New Labour's Top Priority' in Hills *et al. op. cit.*, 71 to 90.

Lupton, R. and Power, A. (2004) *Minority Ethnic Groups in Britain*, CASE, LSE, London.

Lyon, F. and Sepulveda, L. (2009) 'Mapping Social Enterprises: Past Approaches, Challenges and Future Directions', *Social Enterprise Journal*, 5, 83–94.

Marmot, M. (2010) *Fair Society, Healthy Lives*, UCL, London.

Mau, S. (2004) 'Welfare Regimes and the Norms of Social Exchange', *Current Sociology*, 52, 1, 53–74.

Mau. S. and Veghte, B. (2007) *Social Justice, Legitimacy and the Welfare State*, Ashgate, Aldershot.

DOI: 10.1057/9781137328113

Mauss, M. 1990 (1922) *The Gift: Forms and Functions of Exchange in Archaic Societies*, Routledge, London.

Metcalf. D. (2006) *On the Impact of the British National Minimum Wage on Pay and Employment*, WP 1481C, December, School of Economics, LSE, London.

Milkman, R. *et al.* (2012) 'Understanding Occupy', *Contexts*, 11, 2, 12–21.

Mohan, J. (2011) *Mapping the Third Sector*, WP 62, Third Sector Research Centre, University of Southampton.

Moore, A. (2010) 'Outside In: Outsourcing in Government', *Public Finance*, 29 July 2010.

Morel, N., Palier, B. and Palme, J. (2011) *Towards a Social Investment Welfare State?* Policy Press, Bristol.

Morrison, K. and Singer, M. (2007) 'Inequality and Deliberative Development: Revisiting Bolivia's Experience with the PRSP', *Development Policy Review*, 25, 6, 721–40.

NAO (2000) *Management of NHS Productivity*, NAO, London.

NAO (2011) *The Care Quality Commission*, HC 1665, NAO, London.

NAO (2012) *Contract Management of Medical Services*, HC 627, HMSO, London.

NCVO (2010) *The UK Civil Society Almanac 2010*, NCVO, London.

NCVO (2011) *Counting the Cuts: the Impact of Spending Cuts on the UK Voluntary and Community Sector* NCVO, London.

NCVO (2012) *The Work Programme, Perceptions and Experiences of the Voluntary Sector*, NCVO, London.

NEP (2010) *An Anatomy of Economic Inequality in the UK*, Case Report 60, LSE, London.

NHS Litigation Authority (2012) *Factsheet 2*, http://www.nhsla.com/home. htm, accessed 16 February 2013.

Nikolai, R. (2011) 'Mapping the Development of Social Investment Policies', in Morel, N. *et al.* (Eds), *Towards a Social Investment Welfare State?* Policy Press, Bristol.

Niskanen, W. (1994) *Bureaucracy and Public Economics*, Edward Elgar, Cheltenham.

NSPCC (2011) *Payment by Results*, NSPCC, London.

O'Connor, J., Orloff, A. and Shaver, S. (1999) *States, Markets, Families*, Cambridge University Press, Cambridge.

O'Dea, C. (2010) *Who Loses Most From Public Spending Cuts?* IFS, London.

OBR (2010) *Economic and Fiscal Outlook, November 2010*, Cm. 7979, HMSO, London.

DOI: 10.1057/9781137328113

OBR (2011a) *Economic and Fiscal Outlook, November 2011*, Cm. 8218, HMSO, London.

OBR (2011b) *Fiscal Sustainability Report July 2011 – Charts and Tables*, OBR, London.

OBR (2012a) *Economic and Fiscal Outlook*, December 2012, Cm. 8481, HMSO, London.

OBR (2012b) *Forecast Evaluation Report*, October 2012, OBR, London.

OBR (2012c) *Fiscal Sustainability Report*, July 2012, OBR, London.

Observer (2009) *Fraud Inquiry into Government Jobs Scheme*, 28 June.

OECD (2009a) *Viewing the United Kingdom School System through the Prism of PISA*, OECD, Paris.

OECD (2009b) *OECD in Figures*, 2009, OECD, Paris.

OECD (2011a) 'Medium and Long-Term Developments: Challenges and Risks', OECD *Economic Outlook*, 1, Chapter 4.

OECD (2011b) *Privatisation in the 21st Century: Summary of Recent Experiences*, OECD, Paris.

OECD (2011c) *Restoring Public Finances*, OECD, Paris, http://www.oecd.org/governance/budgetingandpublicexpenditures/47558957.pdf, accessed 30 December 2012.

OECD (2012a) *Statextracts*, http://Stats.Oecd.Org/, accessed 16 February 2013.

OECD (2012b) *FDI in Figures*, OECD, Paris.

Ofgem (2012) *Ofgem Statement on Trading in the Gas Market*, http://www.ofgem.gov.uk/pages/moreinformation.aspx?file=gasstatement.pdf&refer=media/pressrel, accessed 16 February 2013.

Oliver, A. (2005) 'The English National Health Service: 1979–2005', *Health Economics*, 14, S75–S99.

ONS (2008 and 2012) *Labour Market Statistics Bulletins*, March 2008 and February 2012, ONS, London.

ONS (2011) *Regional Trends no. 43*, ONS, London.

ONS (2012a) *Social Trends: Households and Families No 41*, ONS, London

ONS (2012b) *Public Sector Employment Q1*, http://www.ons.gov.uk/ons/publications/re-reference-tables.html?edition=tcm%3A77–261324, accessed 16 February 2013.

ONS (2012c) *Working and Workless Households, 2012*, ONS, London.

Orton, M. and Rowlingson, K. (2007) *Public Attitudes to Economic Inequality*, Rowntree Foundation, York.

Osborne, G. (2012) *Speech to Conservative Party Conference*, http://www.newstatesman.com/blogs/politics/2012/10/george-osbornesspeech-conservative-conference-full-text, accessed 30 December 2012.

Palier, B. (2010) *A Long Goodbye to Bismarck?* Amsterdam University Press, Amsterdam.

Palier, B. and Martin, C. (2007) 'From a "Frozen Landscape" to Structural Reforms', *Social Policy and Administration*, 41, 6, 535–54.

Palmer, G. (2011) *The Poverty Site*, http://www.poverty.org.uk/61/index.shtml, accessed 11 January 2013.

Pavolini, E. and Guillen, A. (2013) (Eds) *Public Health Care Systems between Restructuring and Retrenchment*, Palgrave Macmillan, Basingstoke.

Peacock, A. and Wiseman, J. (1967) *The Growth of Public Expenditure in the UK, 1890–1955*, Unwin, London.

Pennycook, M. (2012) *What Price a Living Wage?* IPPR/Resolution Foundation, London.

Peters, R. and 16 Co-Authors (2010) 'The Better Beginnings, Better Futures Project: Findings from Grade 3 to Grade 9', *Monographs in Social Research in Child Development*, 75, 3.

Pickard, L. *et al.* (2012) *Public Expenditure Costs of Carers Leaving Employment*, http://blogs.lse.ac.uk/healthandsocialcare/2012/04/25/dr-linda-pickard-public-expenditure-costs-of-carers-leaving-employment/, accessed 30 December 2012.

Pierson, P. (1994) *Dismantling the Welfare State*, Cambridge University Press, Cambridge.

Pierson, P. (2001) 'Coping with Permanent Austerity', in Paul Pierson (Ed.), *The New Politics of the Welfare State*, Oxford University Press, Oxford.

Potucek, M. (2008) 'Metamorphoses of Welfare States in Central and Eastern Europe', in Seeleib-Kaiser, M. (Ed.), *Welfare State Transformations*, Palgrave Macmillan, Basingstoke.

Prabhakar, R. (2012) 'What Does the Public Think of Taxation?' *Journal of European Social Policy*, 22, 1, 77–89.

Pratchett, L., Durose, C., Lowndes, V., Smith, G., Stoker, G. and Wales, C. (2009) *Empowering Communities*, Department for Communities and Local Government, London.

Propper, C., Sutton, M., Whitnall, C. and Windmeijer, F. (2008) *Incentives and Targets in Hospital Care: Evidence from a Natural Experiment*, WP 08/205, CMPO, University of Bristol.

DOI: 10.1057/9781137328113

PWC (2010) *Sectoral and Regional Impact of the Fiscal Squeeze*, PWC, London.

Ranson, S. *et al.* (2003) 'Parents as Volunteer Citizens', *Parliamentary Affairs*, 56, 716–32.

Richards, P. (2011) 'Back to the Future', in Philpott, R. (Ed.), *Purple Book*, Biteback, London.

Rothstein, B. (2005) *Social Traps and the Problem of Trust*, Cambridge University Press, Cambridge.

Rowlingson, K. and Connor, S. (2011) 'The Deserving Rich? Inequality, Morality and Social Policy', *Journal of Social Policy*, 40, 3, 437–52.

Sassi, F. (2009) 'Tackling Health Inequalities', in Hills, J. and Stewart, K. (Eds), *A More Equal Society? New Labour, Poverty, Inequality and Exclusion*, Policy Press, Bristol.

Schumpeter, J. (1942) *Capitalism, Socialism and Democracy*, Routledge, London.

SCIE (2009) *The Implementation of Individual Budgets in Adult Social Care*, Research Briefing 20, SCIE, London.

SCIE (2011) *Short-Notice Care Home Closures*, SCIE, London.

Scott, S. and Freeman, R. (1995) 'Prevention as a Problem of Modernity: The Example of HIV and AIDS', in Gabe, J. (Ed.), *Medicine, Health and Risk*, Blackwell, Oxford.

Sefton, T. (2005) 'Give and Take', in Park, A. *et al.* (Eds), *British Social Attitudes, 22nd Report*, NATCEN, London.

Sheldrake, J. (1989) *Municipal Socialism*, Avebury, Aldershot.

Skidelsky, R. (2012) *Skidelsky on the Economic Crisis*, Centre For Global Studies, London.

Smith, J. and Naylor, R. (2001) 'Determinants of Degree Performance', *Oxford Bulletin of Economics and Statistics*, 63, 29–60.

Stern, N. (2006) *The Economics of Climate Change*, HM Treasury, London.

Stewart, K. (2007) 'Write the Rules and Win', *Public Administration Review*, November, 1067–76.

Stewart, K. (2009) ' A Scar on the Soul of Society: Child Poverty and Disadvantage under New Labour', in Hills, J., Sefton, T. and Stewart, K. (Eds), *Towards a More Equal Society?: Poverty, Inequality and Policy since 1997*, Policy Press, Bristol.

Stiglitz, J.(2012) *The Price of Inequality*, Norton, New York.

Stoker, G. (2006) *Why Politics Matters*, Palgrave Macmillan, Basingstoke.

Stratton (2010) 'Women Will Bear Brunt of Budget Cuts, Says Yvette Cooper', *Guardian Newspaper*, 4 July.

DOI: 10.1057/9781137328113

Svallfors, S. (2004) 'Class Attitudes and the Welfare State', *Social Policy and Administration*, 38, 2, 119–38.

Svallfors, S. (2007) *The Political Sociology of the Welfare State*, Stanford University Press, Stanford, CA.

Taylor-Gooby, P. (2002) 'The Silver Age of the Welfare State: Perspectives on Resilience', *Journal of Social Policy*, 31, 4, 597–622.

Taylor-Gooby, P. (Ed.) (2004) *New Risks, New Welfare*, Oxford University Press, Oxford.

Taylor-Gooby, P. (2009) *Reframing Social Citizenship*, Oxford University Press, Oxford.

Taylor-Gooby, P. (2012a) 'Root and Branch Restructuring to Achieve Major Cuts: The Social Ambitions of the Coalition', *Social Policy and Administration*, 46, 1, 61–82.

Taylor-Gooby, P. (2012b) 'Public Policy Futures: A Left Trilemma?' *Critical Social Policy*, DOI:10.1177/0261018312458044, accessed 30 December 2012.

Taylor-Gooby, P. (2013) 'Why Do People Stigmatise the Poor at a Time of Rapidly Increasing Inequality, and What Can Be Done about It?' *Political Quarterly*, 84, 1.

Taylor-Gooby, P. and Hastie, C. (2002) 'Support for State Spending', in Park, A. *et al.* (Eds), *British Social Attitudes: The 19th Report*, National Centre for Social Research, London.

Taylor-Gooby, P. and Stoker, G. (2011) 'The Coalition Programme: A New Vision for Britain or Politics as Usual?', *Political Quarterly*, 82, 1, 4–27.

Thompson, J. and Jones, A. (2012) 'RSB Set for Talks to Settle Libor Claims', *Financial Times*, 1 November.

Timonen, V. (2003) *Restructuring the Welfare State*, Edward Elgar, Cheltenham.

Titmuss, R. (1955) 'The Social Division of Welfare', in *Essays on the Welfare State*, Allen and Unwin, London.

Titmuss, R. (1970) *The Gift Relationship*, Penguin Books, Harmondsworth.

Townsend, P. (1982) (with Davidson, N.) *Inequalities in Health*, Penguin, London.

Van Oorschot, W. (2000) 'Who Should Get What, and Why? On Deservingness Criteria and the Conditionality of Solidarity among the Public', *Policy & Politics*, 28, 1, 33–48.

Van Oorschot, W. (2006) 'Making the Difference in Social Europe: Deservingness Perceptions among Citizens of European Welfare States' *Journal of European Social Policy*, 16, 1, 23–42.

DOI: 10.1057/9781137328113

Vanderbrouke, F., Hemerijk, A. and Palier, B. (2011) *Why the EU Needs a Social Investment Pact*, Opinion Paper No 5, OSE, Brussels.

Walshe, K. (2010) *Reorganisation of the NHS in England*, BMJ, 341:C3843.

Ward-Batts, J. (2008) 'Out of the Wallet and into the Purse: Using Microdata to Test Income Pooling', *Journal of Human Resources*, 43, 2, 325–51.

Whittaker, M. (2012) *Squeezed Britain?* Resolution Foundation, http://www.resolutionfoundation.org/publications/essential-guide-squeezed-britain/, accessed 30 December 2012.

Wilson, D. (2010) *Targets, Choice and Voice*, 2020 Public Services Trust, RSA, London.

WBG (2011a) *The Impact on Women of the 2011 Budget*, WBG, London.

WBG (2011b) *Universal Credit, WBG Briefing*, WBG, London.

WBG (2012a) *Plan A Has Failed; It Is Time for Plan F*, WBG, London.

WBG (2012b) *The Impact on Women of the Autumn Financial Statement 2012 and the Welfare Benefits Uprating Bill 2013*, WBG, London.

Yeates, N. *et al.* (2011) *In Defence of Welfare*, Social Policy Association, Lincoln.

YouGov (2012) *Yougov Tracker*, Yougov, London.

YPLA (2010) *16–19 Funding Statement*, Young Peoples' Learning Agency, London.

DOI: 10.1057/9781137328113

Index

DOI: 10.1057/9781137328113

DOI: 10.1057/9781137328113

DOI: 10.1057/9781137328113

Lightning Source UK Ltd.
Milton Keynes UK
UKOW041139040613

211741UK00001B/4/P